Against
the Current

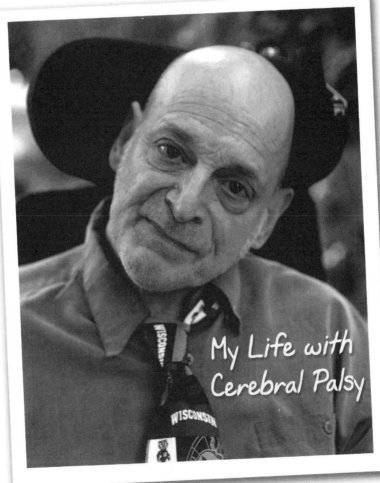

My Life with
Cerebral Palsy

**FULL
COURT
Press**

BOB SEGALMAN

P.O. Box 930160
Verona, Wisconsin 53593-0160 USA
Phone 800-327-4269   Fax 800.942.3865

www.AttainmentCompany.com

©2009 Attainment Company, Inc.

Library of Congress Cataloging-in-Publication Data

Printed in the United States of America

Author: Bob Segalman, Ph.D., SC.D. (Hon.)
Editors: Linda Schreiber, MS, CCC-SLP
        Tom Kinney
Cover Photo: Kristel Durand

ISBN 1-57861-675-1

Dedication

To my father, Professor Ralph Segalman (1916–2008), whose love, foresight, encouragement, assertiveness, and "kvetching" had a strong positive influence on my success

and

to everyone with a speech disability who can benefit from increased telephone access through Speech-to-Speech.

Contents

Preface

When Linda Schreiber, my editor, asked me to write about why I am writing this book, all I could think about was sixth grade. My teacher then, Mrs. Kipp, asked me to write about my summer vacation. She was so upset when I gave two pages about kissing Mary Jones in back of the garage that she called Mom—who had trouble not laughing during the conversation.

I have to admit that having a strong ego can stimulate writing an autobiography. I am sure many of my old girlfriends will tell you that I have an ego as big as Chicago. Of course, now that the population of Los Angeles exceeds the population of Chicago, that comment needs to be updated.

The idea for this book began right after I took my first government job and I was looking for something to do between nine and five (after I finished the three hours of work that each of us was assigned daily). I took enough notes to write the book back in 1973, but just about then, my agency hired an efficiency expert who found other things to do with my time. Thus, my notes for this book went back on the shelf.

The State of California was not very good about hiring time and motion consultants (efficiency experts) on an ongoing basis. Over my 30 year career, I've found time available to write many articles about my life experiences with cerebral palsy (CP). This book contains some of that writing. For its lack of consistency in hiring efficiency experts, the readers of this book should be grateful to the State of California. Parenthetically, my brother Dan read the draft of this paragraph and assures me that the civil servants with whom he has collaborated work against this stereotype.

The proceeds from this book will go to Speech Communications Assistance by Telephone, Inc. SCT is a nonprofit organization (501c3, FIN 68-0217675), dedicated to promoting telephone assistance to people with speech disabilities. SCT grew from

Preface

my work to establish a national telephone assistance service for people with speech disabilities, called Speech-to-Speech. You can find "more than you'll ever want to know" about Speech-to-Speech later in this book.

I hope that my editor, Linda, is happier with this preface than Mrs. Kipp was with my description of my summer vacation.

Acknowledgments

Just as it takes a whole village to raise a child, it takes many people to make the life of anyone with a severe disability successful. Hundreds of people made my life better. To list any individual would be to leave someone out. Thanks to everybody who made my life better. Thanks to the all the villagers who helped raise this child.

Chronology

1942—Born

1943—Moved to Tucson, AZ for six months and then to
Springfield, IL

1944—Began to crawl

1945—Moved to Chicago

1947—Moved to Sioux City, IA

1948—Began first grade in Sioux City, IA

1953—Moved to Waterbury, CT

1957—Graduated eighth grade and began high school

1961—Graduated high school and moved to El Paso, TX

1964—First diagnosed with depression, controlled
with medication

1965—Graduated from college and moved to Tallahassee, FL

1966—Finished master's of science degree and moved
to Madison, WI

1972—Finished Ph.D. and began work with the State of
California at Pacific (Lanterman) State Hospital
(Developmental Center) in Pomona

1973—Learned to drive a car

1975—Started using a power wheelchair

1978—Married

1979—Began work at the Bureau of Criminal Statistics in
Sacramento, CA

Chronology

1989—Hip fused

1989-1996—Served on the California Relay Service
　　　　　Advisory Committee

1995—First Speech-to-Speech Trial (STS) in California

1998—Gave STS presentation before Federal Communications
　　　　Commission (FCC)

2000—Texas began STS with Sprint; Australia began
　　　　　providing STS; Sweden conducted a national trial

2001—STS began nationwide by FCC mandate; provided
　　　　STS training in Hawaii and Australia

2003—Lectured on STS in Germany

2004—Retired from the State of California

2005—Speech Communication Assistance by Telephone, Inc.,
　　　　was founded as a national, consumer-driven
　　　　organization in the USA

2006—Received Honorary Doctor of Science,
　　　　　University of Wisconsin

2007—Moved to my own apartment

Introduction

Clop, Clop

It is 2008. The sunshine bounces off my clean, white walls. I am happy; happy with myself, happy to have time alone—with lots of room in this crowded world.

A horse and carriage goes by on Sacramento's P Street, probably with young lovers inside. I hope that they are happy. I wish them a good life, a few children, lots of education, meaningful and secure employment, maximized 401(k)s, common interests, common values, and common sense.

Clop, Clop

It is 1946. A horse waits while our train goes by in southern Illinois. I am just 3 and excited to be going to see grandmother in Peoria. Dad sings to Mom, "Passengers will please refrain from flushing toilets while the train is standing in the station. I love you."

Clop, Clop

It is 1948. Truman just beat Dewey. I watch the beer company horses parade by in downtown Sioux City, Iowa, on the day I start first grade. I don't know that I am making history. I am the first child with a disability to attend regular school classes in Sioux City—maybe in all of Iowa. A few years later, black students at Little Rock High School will make history too, in some ways different, but in many ways similar.

Clop, Clop

It is 1953. Dad is ambitious. The car radio announces a cease-fire in Korea. Dad pulls the car to the side of the Pennsylvania highway, so my sister, brother, and I can watch the horses grazing. Our family is driving to Waterbury, Connecticut, where Dad will begin his second job as a social work agency executive.

Clop, Clop

It is 1958. I am 15. Grandfather takes me horseback riding. The horse goes under a tree branch and slowly pushes me off her back, introducing me to passive-aggressive revenge.

Clop, Clop

In November 1961, there are horses on the Waterbury, Connecticut, town green, surrounded by a large crowd waiting to hear John F. Kennedy speak. We stand in the cold until his 1 a.m. address; I'm a thrilled high school senior!

Clop, Clop

It is 1963. I am eating lunch in the college cafeteria and listening to "Pretty Horses" over the loudspeaker. Suddenly, the music stops and the dean announces JFK's death. Later, I trudge across the campus of the University of Texas at El Paso from my zoology class. My heart is as heavy as my briefcase. The friend walking with me weeps, quietly.

Clop, Clop

In 1966, we drive down narrow roads near Florida State University in Tallahassee, where I am completing a master's degree. We pass the university farm and see horses grazing. In contrast to my high anxiety as I struggle with advanced statistics, I admire how calm the horses are.

Clop, Clop

It is a December day in 1969. The horses at the other end of the barn whinny impatiently for food, as I watch the farmer finish his milking chores while a Strauss waltz plays over the university radio station. The impatient horses remind me of the impatient students on campus protesting the war in Vietnam. I am writing my doctoral dissertation at the University of Wisconsin–Madison.

Clop, Clop

It is 1979. I have finished 7 years as a social worker near Los Angeles and I am about to begin 13 years as a statistician with California's Bureau of Criminal Statistics. We stop as horses pass on a rural highway. I'm moving to Sacramento, the capitol of California; what a big shot I am!

Clop, Clop

It is 1995. The ocean looks big as I gaze across the Port of Lisbon and listen to horses in the background. My conference has ended; my talk went well. That day I visited Portugal's home for people with multiple disabilities. People much like me, but with no education, no employment, and no hope. As I ache for them, I realize my good fortune.

Clop, Clop

It is 2001. I am training operators to revoice on behalf of Australians with speech disabilities, so they have access to the telephone. Both my friend and a koala bear wait patiently as a horse passes in front of the photographer. We are at "Dreamworld" in Brisbane.

Clop, Clop

It is 2003. While telephone system trials go well, German consumers with speech disabilities are not strong enough to convince the government to establish a permanent service. I am disappointed. Berlin's cold November wind chills us.

We pause to watch marching horses as we make our way to Germany's telecommunications commission headquarters.

Clop, Clop

It is 2006. Back in Madison to receive an honorary doctorate for my work on telephone access, I think about that Madison farmer and his hungry horses. I am now the only known American with CP to hold two doctorates.

Later that same year, New Zealand announces a trial of this telephone service. Perhaps I can do training and see horses there. My new speech generating device will make giving these trainings easier.

A horse-drawn carriage goes by on P Street. Our Quiddler game just finished. It is bedtime. Life is good.

Professor Joe Elder and Bob's dad at a party celebrating Bob's honorary doctorate in 2006.

Chapter One
Childhood

Many aspects of my life were predetermined by the hypoxia that occurred before and/or during birth, which resulted in cerebral palsy. This condition limited my speech and ambulation. This book documents how my family and I responded to this limitation. Our response produced positive results far beyond anyone's expectation.

My Birth and Early Years
Birth to 6 years

Missive: This article was written by my mother, Anita Segalman, around 1990 and is a reflection of my first six years of life.

Bob was born December 4, 1942, in Peoria, Illinois. My relatives had gathered on December 3rd at my parent's house in Peoria to celebrate family birthdays.

During the party, I went into labor. In those days, doctors still made house calls. Dr. Morris Adland came to the house and confirmed labor had indeed begun. The doctor recommended that Bob's father (Ralph), go to Methodist Hospital. My mother went with us.

In the delivery room, Dr. Adland was dissatisfied with the nature of the contractions and gave me a shot to increase them. Bob was born in the early hours of the morning, but he did not breathe. Dr. Adland told the nurse to put me under, so he could work with the baby and so I would stop asking questions. When I awoke and asked for my baby, whom I wanted to nurse, I was told he could not suckle and he would stay in the nursery, but they would bring him to me for 10 minutes every day at 6:00 p.m. The nurses fed him with a bottle that had large holes in the nipple. Bob and I were kept at the hospital for 10 days.

One day, a nurse came into the room and told me that my baby had had a cerebral hemorrhage. When I mentioned it to Dr. Adland, he denied it. That was only the first of many denials. In later years, Dr. Adland also denied having delivered Bob. Bob later obtained his legal and official birth certificates with the doctor's signature.

When Bob was 10 or 12 years old, visiting my parents in Peoria, he saw a physical medicine specialist. That doctor read records of Bob's birth in the hospital. He said it was longer than 5 minutes before Bob was breathing on his own; thank goodness Dr. Adland had not discontinued the artificial respiration.

Shortly after Bob's birth, the United Service Organization (USO) gave Ralph an assignment in Tucson, Arizona. Since he would eventually have responsibilities all over the state, they issued him a car to drive there. Later, Bob and I joined him. It was a long train ride.

Ralph found a small house in the country that had once been a chicken coop. It had been nicely remodeled, and its windows opened onto the surrounding farm. One day, a horse looked in the window. The true question became who was more surprised: the horse or the occupants? I often left Bob with the neighboring farm family and traveled to Phoenix, Douglas, Prescott, and other military bases with Ralph.

In June 1943, Ralph got notice from his Peoria draft board to report for his army physical in Chicago. We went back to live with my parents in Peoria. The draft board doctors could not decide if Ralph was well enough to be drafted. They gave him a suspended 1-A. He was to report again in three months.

USO's Jewish Welfare Board sent Ralph to Camp Campbell on the Tennessee-Kentucky border; not a good place to spend summer in the days before air conditioning. The second draft board physical exam produced a 4-F—unfit for service. There were unidentifiable spots on Ralph's lungs, and the draft board staff had filled their quota for the day.

In November 1943, we moved to Springfield, Illinois, where Ralph was director of the Jewish Federation. He visited state agencies looking for help for Bob. In February 1944, when Bob was 14 months old, a woman at one of these agencies told him about Dr. Meyer Perlstein. (Dr. Perlstein later became nationally known for his work in CP.) Dr. Perlstein ran a diagnostic clinic

at St. John's Children's Hospital in Springfield. The woman didn't know whether or not that would be helpful to us; neither did we, but Ralph asked her to make an appointment for us.

Perlstein and his wife, a dermatologist, were both at the examining table. He asked if Bob said sounds with specific meaning. Yes, we were aware of eight. "Then," said Dr. Perlstein, "he has normal intelligence." When he held Bob up on the table, there was reciprocal motion of his legs. Dr. Perlstein said that he would walk, but he could not say when. Before we left, one of the nuns who assisted Dr. Perlstein gave us two or three mimeographed sheets of exercises to do with Bob. The information from that examination formed the basis of my goal: that Bob would become physically, financially, and emotionally independent. Many seemingly minor future decisions were based on that. Friends and neighbors sometimes disapproved of activities we permitted Bob to do, but we stood our ground in maintaining our goals.

In June of 1944, at the age of 18 months, Bob had not yet begun to crawl; but he did scoot along the floor on his belly. On June 6, 1944, he pulled himself up on the rungs of his highchair and stood for a moment. Spectacular for telling, but never repeated. In the fall of 1944, Dr. Perlstein suggested I find housing in Chicago, so I could take Bob to the studio of Anne Rudolph, a dancer who was doing experimental physical therapy (PT) with children like Bob. She was teaching children to get off their abdomens and crawl on their hands and knees. The goal for the children was to climb the painted pumpkins on the floor. She thought it important for them to experiment riding, to feel the weight on their feet. Another technique she used was to wrap a sheet around their middles; she attached each end of the sheet to the opposing wall, about six feet away from each child in each direction. She put a table of toys in front of them. Sometimes she held them up with a wrapped sheet and had them walk about the room.

These lessons lasted an hour or two, several times a week, for a few months. I found the waiting room less attractive than the Chicago Museum of Art, one block south and across Michigan Boulevard. When we returned home, Bob scooted about the apartment in a stroller with the footrest and long handle removed. On April 12, 1945, while we wept at the death of Franklin Delano Roosevelt, Ralph installed a railing down the length of the long hallway that separated the kitchen from the rest of the apartment. Bob could cling to it and walk.

Bob came to know PT intensely. Forty years later, Bob would comment, "Physical therapists would be perfectly content if you did nothing else in your life besides go to PT and do your exercises."

After the war in Europe ended, the Joint Distribution Committee asked Ralph if he would come to Europe to work with refugees. It was agreed that if Bob could be admitted to the CP nursery school at Michael Reese Hospital (which I had visited the previous year when it was first established), Ralph would go to Europe for a year. Bob was admitted and Ralph went to Europe. Bob's grandparents were very helpful to us during Ralph's absence, then, as always. In August, I went to Chicago and applied for housing. We got a one-bedroom apartment on Kimbark at 52nd Street, two blocks from one cousin's apartment. We also lived within walking distance of two other cousins and my brother who was a student at the University of Chicago. We were surrounded with the support of family.

We were also six blocks from Lake Michigan. I often pushed Bob there in our newly molded stroller that had a fiberglass seat. Bob continued to crawl as his mode of movement. Friends in the building wondered why I permitted him to get so dirty crawling around the apartment. My mother gave me a small sewing machine for patching the knees of his trousers. Bob continued to crawl; self-directed and independent.

Bob was 3 in December 1945, and he needed and enjoyed the companionship of other children. He liked going to visit family and friends. Ralph came home that September. During the winter, Ralph worked for the Jewish Family Service and with arriving refugees in Douglas Park; he had a miserable commute.

In the fall of 1947, we moved to Sioux City, Iowa. We rented an old, two-story white frame house on what would later become the parking lot of the Jewish Community Center. The house preceded indoor plumbing. The bathroom was an add-on, two steps down, and on the second floor. It was at 1409 Nebraska Street, across from the fire station where, a year later, Bob watched voters in the Truman-Dewey election.

There were no educational facilities for Bob in Sioux City; Ralph invented one in a rented school building to serve as the temporary Jewish Community Center. Ralph found a teacher through the Easter Seals Foundation who was interested in working with children who had CP. He also found five or six children about Bob's age who had similar needs. Bob's short stay in this setting would be his first primary experience in a classroom with other children with disabilities. The teacher said she had never seen a child who wanted to learn how to read as much as did Bob. Ralph talked with the school social worker and psychologist. They met Bob and agreed he belonged in a traditional classroom.

Kindergarten was not an appropriate place for Bob. The social worker interviewed the first-grade teachers to find one who was comfortable having Bob in her class, and they discovered Alice Erskine at Irving School (many schools in Sioux City were named after famous writers). She had a slow-moving class that would spend two years covering, not repeating, first grade. Her class would give Bob time to begin to walk independently and for his speech to become familiar to the staff and children. When Bob entered school, he was given a probationary period because of his disability. Miss Erskine prepared the children for Bob's arrival in October, explaining that he could not do all the things they could do, but that he could do many things that they could not yet do, such as tell time.

I accompanied Bob to school his first few weeks to revoice his words and to hold his hand for support on the playground. He attended class the first half of the morning and the first half of the afternoon, with a nap in between at home for the first few weeks. I pulled him to and from school in his wagon until winter approached. Then we bought a 1936 Plymouth. By December, his six probationary weeks were over and he became a full-time student.

It was time for another child. Ruth was born September 12, 1949. In the spring of 1950, we moved to 517 South Irene Street in a different part of town, where Bob could walk the two or three blocks to school. His third-grade teacher was a gem. He had friends at school and among the children who lived across the street. About that time, he began to spend summers with his grandparents in Peoria. That summer pattern continued until he graduated from high school.

In the fall of 1950, Bob and Ruth stayed with their grandparents in Peoria while Ralph and I vacationed at Turkey Run State Park in Indiana. While in Peoria, Ruth learned to walk and Bob attended a special education class. He said he would never be adequately prepared for college if he had to go to that school all the time. That is, Bob thought that the education provided in that class was not rigorous enough for children to receive the sufficient core subject matter instruction needed to succeed in a mainstream academic environment.

A Younger Brother and Sister

Chronology:

Bob born	1942
Ruth born	1949
Dan born	1952

First-Born Son

In a family that highly valued both intellectuality and maleness, I was an intelligent first-born son. In addition to those advantages, for the first seven years of my life I was an only child. Thus, my parents had the time and energy to devote to meeting my crucial early medical and developmental needs. They provided, for example, daily physical and speech therapy at home on the days I had no clinic services.

During those early years, I developed the psychological resources of many "only" children. My social needs were and are few; I have grown into my 40s* content to spend much of my time alone with my computer, just as I used to spend it with my Lincoln Logs and American Bricks as a child or with my ham radio as a teenager. Perhaps those resources, combined with social isolation common to those with speech impairments, allowed me to develop the concentration necessary to complete a Ph.D. and sustain a research career.

Rivalry

My sister Ruth was born just a year after I began attending regular classes as a first grader in a neighborhood school. (The process of integrating children with disabilities into regular classes was later called "mainstreaming" and is now called placement "in the least restrictive environment" or "full inclusion.") Mom had trouble becoming pregnant until

I was accepted into school. Psychologically, she may have been afraid to try to manage a second child since she had the sole responsibility of educating me at home. If that were not enough, they also worried about how I would accept a younger sibling. For that reason, my parents told me to look forward to Ruth's birth, as I was to receive gifts, have more privileges as a "big brother," and be one step closer to adulthood.

My parents hoped that being a big brother might enhance my self-image as well as compensate for any loss of self-image that I had related to my disability. That is what happened. Because Ruth was a girl, I may have gained additional confidence from the sexist values of the day. Two and a half years later, my brother Dan was born. Ruth is roughly seven years younger than me, Dan is almost ten.

How could I be jealous of siblings so much younger than I? Somehow I managed. Mom was changing the diaper on Ruth's seven-month-old bottom, when I lay down next to her and imitated the pose. Mom said that whatever sibling rivalry Ruth and I experienced disappeared when Dan was born. Had Ruth, Dan, and I been closer in age, much more jealousy would most likely have arisen.

I'm glad the jealous feelings I had were so close to the surface; some children with disabilities express their rivalry by subconsciously exacerbating their medical condition to gain parental attention. As it was, my parents already had reason enough to be more concerned about my health, my career, and my well-being than about Ruth's and Dan's.

But as children and teenagers, they did not seem jealous. For example, one year Dad and Mom relocated to help me with my Ph.D. dissertation. Dad insisted that Dan move with them and spend his senior year at a new high school, which Dan felt limited his academic opportunities drastically. Although Dan was furious with Dad, he was never upset with me.

I coped with what little sibling rivalry there was by pretending it was not there. That is how I handled many problems (from painful leg braces to crab grass) and that is probably one key to my success. Whether this is "denial" or not, it works. I am occasionally jealous because Dan's Ph.D. is in the physical sciences, while mine is in the social sciences. I do, however, recognize these feelings as irrational. When my brother read a draft of this paragraph, he teased me again about this.

Like all brothers, we made the usual comparisons of sexual exploits with claims and counterclaims throughout the years. However, as we entered middle age and the primary function of sex became an opportunity for continued closeness with long-time spouses, even these rivalries faded. What's left of our sibling rivalry comes out in jokes about who is publishing the most—a senseless, but mutually enjoyable, bantering. (Upon reading this paragraph, my brother joked that I "had an active sex life" back then, but that he was "an engineering student." I beg to differ!)

Big Brother

From the time of their births, I have always had warm and protective feelings toward Ruth, Dan, and now toward their families—a protectiveness that my parents have always encouraged. At age 11, I began to baby-sit them and by 12 or 13, I escorted Ruth on a cross-country airplane trip with parents on the sending end and grandparents on the receiving end.

Sometimes, it was difficult to be a big brother and a teenager at the same time. My baby sitting responsibilities occasionally included finding a replacement if I wanted to go out the same night as Mom and Dad. Although I dated rarely in high school, I was embarrassed one night to find that the sitter I had obtained was the best friend of the girl with whom I had a date. I worried that the two girls might talk about me behind my back!

Another baby sitting problem was that my brother (now an engineer) enjoyed disassembling things and I had to supervise him closely, since I lacked the manual dexterity to reassemble his projects. I was reminded of this last year when he had the gear box of my power wheelchair strewn over his hotel room floor and was unsure, momentarily, how to put it back together.

I was not always a reliable big brother. At age 12, I stopped to talk to a friend on a walk to the mailbox; I finished talking and started to walk away, backwards, as Mom sometimes did. Unfortunately, I had walked backwards into the street with Dan in tow, when we were both hit by a truck. Luckily, neither of us was permanently injured.

Ruth says that I was unusually patient with her and attributes this patience to the expected role of the older brother and to the patience I learned living with CP. I spent hours teaching her Morse code, going over every letter until she could recognize it. As a finale, I tapped out one long phrase that I knew she would understand and that would give her self-confidence. I was very disappointed that she did not understand when I tapped out: "The refrigerator is cold," until I realized that I had omitted the pauses between the words!

One problem with assuming some parental responsibility at age 7 is that from then on I criticized every move my parents made. I nagged Mom not to be too strict with Dan, but my dire predictions about how it would ruin him never came to pass.

Our age differences, along with several family moves, gave Ruth and Dan the advantage of not having many of the same teachers as I did. The high visibility of elder-disabled siblings can leave reputations for their younger siblings to either live up to or overcome. Fortunately for Ruth, she told me that her teachers always spoke very highly of me.

Ruth and Dan have always been helpful; perhaps as children, being helpful gave them an excuse to be around their older brother. For me this has been nice, yet such helpfulness could lead a person with a disability into an unhealthy dependency.

Because my injury was at birth, my parents were cautious about having more children and unusually anxious about the births of my siblings. Dan, initially a shallow breather, prompted "I told you so's" from interfering relatives. The decision to have other children after having a child with a disability is always complex, but for my parents, the advantages far outweighed the disadvantages. Ruth and Dan have enriched all of our lives in untold ways.

Just Brothers and Sister

Our relationships differed little from those of children from families without a child with a disability. Any problems or special circumstances that arose are difficult to identify. For a child, life is just life; and without experience living as an able-bodied person, I cannot tell how our relationships might have differed. With Ruth and Dan around, the attention focused less on me. This was beneficial. Smothering is a "developmental hazard" of people with disabilities.

In oral communication, our relationships closely resemble those of able-bodied offspring. Ruth and Dan have listened to me speak since their birth, so they understand me more readily than others. I enjoy phoning them, even when I am tired, since I know communication will be easy. Similarly, my parents were often asked if they were concerned that Ruth or Dan might have picked up my speech patterns, but that was never a problem. (Dan reminded me that when he was young, he had a developmental speech problem which had nothing to do with my speech.) Amusingly, the only one who successfully imitated my speech was a graduate school buddy who did a hilarious imitation of me defending my dissertation orally.

My own perception of my disability facilitated my relationships with everyone around me including Ruth and Dan. In spite of being told that I walked awkwardly and that people had trouble understanding my speech, I never thought of myself as disabled until I was an adult. Younger brothers and sisters pick up older siblings' values, and Ruth and Dan followed my lead with Mom and Dad's encouragement. A further reason that the three of us did not take the "differentness" of my disability that seriously was that being Jews made us all "different." I was just "more different."

When a school teacher told Ruth that caring for and raising me must have been difficult for Mom, Ruth did not know what the teacher meant. Ruth was in high school when she realized that it must have been a struggle for me to learn to walk and talk.

Fortunately, Ruth and Dan were raised not to worry about me. Generally, my parents did not allow my disability to disturb family life. For example, Ruth remembers that Mom took her to the library when I went to speech therapy three blocks away. While the neighbor girl's library trips were coordinated with her brother's little league practice, Ruth did not mind that hers were coordinated with my speech therapy. Such efforts to make all our lives as normal as possible benefited me in the long run.

A Final Word

I was a child with a speech and ambulation disability, born into a middle class family with only typical sibling conflict. I completed my education, had a successful career, and enjoyed marriage. There were problems along the way, but they were overcome or circumvented. Advantages I had as a child included: my intellect; birth order; and loving, prodding, dedicated, and innovative parents. They valued intellectual achievement and I made the most of the situation. I am grateful that Ruth and Dan played a part in this process.

*Just to clarify, this story was written when I was in my 40s, but I am including it in this book, which I am publishing at age 65. Many chapters were written in my 30s, 40s, and 50s.

This article was first published in September of 1990 in Contact, *the magazine of the Canadian CP Association (published in French and English); then republished in December of 1991 in* The Parents for Special Children Newsletter, *Sacramento, CA. Reprinted with permission.*

First Grade

Age 6

In October 1948, one month before Truman beat Dewey and more than 25 years before federal law guaranteed an education to children with disabilities, I became the first child with a significant disability in Sioux City, Iowa to attend classes for children who are able-bodied. Born with CP, I could walk leaning on others and could talk, even though only Mom, Dad, and a few others could understand me.

At that time, in Sioux City, children with disabilities either attended special classes or received home instruction; but the school social worker, Mrs. Bowers, promised to help find a mainstream class for me to attend. My father was the director of the Sioux City Jewish Federation and had helped some of her clients, so she was glad to help me in return.

I was almost 6 and was very interested in starting school. I could read a little and remember nagging Mom to teach me more. Before she met Miss Erskine who was interested in having me in her class, Miss Bowers had spoken to several first-grade teachers in neighborhood schools. Miss Erskine had just the right kind of class for me; hers was slower than all the other first-grade classrooms at Irving School. This class would take two school years to complete first-grade work. During that time, I was the highest scoring pupil, a compensating benefit for a child with a disability.

I started school in October and must have known that I had to sell myself. On Halloween I gave everyone in the class a card and had Mom put a stick of gum in each one. When anyone asked me about my walking I said, "I can't walk well, but I can tell time." I would then show them Grandfather's big pocket watch and explain how to read it. They soon forgot about my walking.

When I began school, I attended only two hours a day so I would have time to get used to the routine, and so the other children could get accustomed to the unusual child in their midst. I got tired at first, but gradually my stamina grew and within six weeks I was able to attend all day. Mom stayed with me in class all the time, at first just to translate my speech for Miss Erskine, but Mom's attendance became less necessary as Miss Erskine began to understand me and as I began to do well academically.

A month or so into the term, Mom no longer needed to come with me. Regardless, all through school, Mom took the initiative in getting to know each of my teachers and encouraging them to call at the onset of any problem. I never felt awkward about this, as it just seemed to be another dimension of my special circumstance.

My success in first grade gave my parents enormous joy. They saw it both as a signal of my eventual independence, both physical and financial, and as evidence that they would not need to educate me at home. For me, this first year was the onset of a completely mainstreamed education.

Because so few pupils with disabilities were mainstreamed then, there were few opportunities for me to meet them. In grade school, I rarely met other pupils with disabilities and often wondered if any existed. I met a few at summer camps for children with disabilities. Since I hated being patronized, however, I always left those camps after a few days. The greater majority of those children were educationally or intellectually challenged, leaving us little in common.

Once, when I visited my grandparents in Peoria for two weeks, I attended a special class for children with orthopedic handicaps. Much time was wasted in naps and arts and crafts with very little actual academic instruction. I spent the entire two weeks worrying that I would fall behind in my class at home. I had a similar experience when I spent two weeks at a rehabilitation center during my junior year of high school.

My teachers had written out detailed, daily homework assignments. For the two weeks of the rehabilitation program, I would stay up until 11 p.m. each evening to finish my homework. Sadly, the staff started giving me tranquilizers. They viewed my industriousness as neurosis. Throughout my life, many people around me have viewed my tremendous drive in a similar way. I have always needed to push on, despite such detractors. I am lucky that I seem to have inherited Dad's need to be assertive as he was the youngest of five children in a very poor family. Thus, he was forced to become assertive at a very young age in order to get his fair share of the meager offerings at the dinner table.

Throughout high school and college, I was the only student with disabilities. I grew up as the only different one wherever I went; that helped prepare me for a life of employment as the only person with a disability in my work-unit, as I usually was.

None of my teachers had taught a child with a disability before, and I attended school before teachers' colleges developed special education curricula. Thus, I had the advantage of being judged on my merits rather than on arbitrary standards or on the performance of pupils with challenges who preceded me. I was lucky to have been placed in a mainstream class, where I was forced to work up to my potential.

My long-term ambitions were still greater than those which many of my teachers had for me. This was because their understanding of my disability was different than my actual

experience and ability. People told me that I was disabled, that my speech was slurred, and that my walk was clumsy and slow. Yet when I spoke, I heard the words in my head as I said them, so they sounded clear to me. My walk seemed slow to me, but it did not seem clumsy, as I always looked straight ahead and could not see my legs twisting. With my strong self-confidence, I could not understand how my disability might block success.

This article was first published in January of 1989 in the DLE Update, *Sacramento, CA; then republished in January of 1990 in* Mainstream Magazine, *San Diego, CA. Reprinted with permission.*

Dad's Geography Lessons
Ages 0 to 22

Because my father was ambitious as a young man, our family moved each time he got the opportunity for a better job. With each move, I got a taste of a new way of living or a different part of the country. Every place we lived had something different to offer.

The first lesson started in Peoria, Illinois where I was born in 1942. Peoria was the world center of tractor manufacturing, and the headquarters of Hiram Walker Whiskey. There was a local joke that many Peorians were arrested annually for DUI (driving under the influence) while driving a tractor. At one time, five of my Peoria cousins each owned a different neighborhood clothing store there. Anyone who feuded with my family went naked.

After moves to Tucson, Arizona and Springfield, Illinois, we moved to Chicago. There I learned something about big city living, even though I was only 3 years old. One thing I did not learn in Chicago was my colors. The "Yellow Cabs" that took us to nursery school were painted orange, and it took me several years to get those two colors straight in my head. We went to a nursery school in Chicago that taught us to be good sports, ostensibly so we would be devoted Cubs fans.

Dad's geography lessons continued with a move to Sioux City, Iowa (in 1948), which then had the country's fifth–largest stockyards. They smelled so bad that the city fathers built a mile-long bridge over them. Another large industry there was honey manufacturing and processing. I suggested to my fourth-grade class that the city should install giant sprays on the honey plants to inundate the stockyards and neutralize their smell.

Dad taught us about New England's geography when he took a job in Waterbury, Connecticut, when I was 10 (in 1953). For every cow that came to Sioux City, Waterbury made a brass bell to hang around its neck. As the brass capitol of the world, it was full of noisy, smelly foundries. We have two large brass ashtrays as souvenirs. I still annoy my mother by banging them together on her coffee table to the tune of the Yellow Rose of Texas.

Speaking of Texas, Dad moved us to El Paso in 1961, the year I began college. El Paso is a hot, dry, West Texas town, where we lived while I attended the University of Texas at El Paso. My

ego thrived, as I joined many college organizations and became a Big Man on Campus at this then-small college. I enjoyed being a big fish in a small pond. Of course, I had to use tons of deodorant to control my fishy smell.

One good thing about all this moving around is that no one I know now remembers my youthful pranks. During my working years, I didn't have to worry about rolling down the corridors of my office building and meeting people from my past. I never saw my neighbor from my high school days who caught me stealing his hubcaps, or his gorgeous daughter who put me up to it.

That is the end of Dad's geography lessons. Later, I moved on my own; first to sweat in Florida and then to freeze in Wisconsin—just for a graduate education—but that is another story.

This article was first published in May of 1991 in DLE Update, *Sacramento, CA. Reprinted with permission.*

A Superb Teacher

Age 12

Everyone should be lucky enough to have one superb teacher during their school years. For me, it was my sixth–and seventh–grade teacher, Mrs. Kipp. She was probably 35 when I first entered her classroom about 1955, but to this 12-year-old boy, "she seemed old." She had to be old, because she remembered stories of World War I. Also, she recalled her mother's memory of the blizzard of 1888, and her father's experience helping to build the Panama Canal.

Her vivid descriptions of history verified her antiquity. We incorrectly credited her with being the first person to say that "the Holy Roman Empire was neither Holy, Roman, nor an Empire." We also thought that she invented the description of "Russia's three great generals who defeated Napoleon: General Vastness, General Cold, and General Mud." We assumed that she lived through the demise of both the Holy Roman Empire and Napoleon.

Mrs. Kipp probably influenced my career choice by fostering my love of both writing and numbers. Her only homework assignment was to turn in a book report every Monday morning. For the life of me, I can't remember any of the 30 books I reported on for her, but I can sure remember struggling with those book reports as the year went on. Writing those book reports also gave me extensive typing experience, which has held me in good stead. Dad dragged that huge ancient electric typewriter up our three flights of stairs, so that I would not have to write my book reports in longhand. Despite his grumbling, his kindness could be wonderful.

As for numbers, Mrs. Kipp conveyed to us her love of long division 20 years before hand calculators became commonplace. I too liked long division, but she never could teach me to keep all my numbers on the page; every time I divided, the remainder moved farther to the right, and inevitably I had to write the final remainder in the right margin. My able-bodied classmates had trouble keeping their columns in order, but with my dexterity difficulties, the challenge was even greater.

Another problem I had with arithmetic stemmed from Mrs. Kipp's incentive system. Making As three days in a row excused you from arithmetic class for two weeks. Even though I enjoyed working with numbers, I always received a B on the third day. Without exception, I scrupulously checked Mrs. Kipp's grading on the third day. You see, I suspected that she just gave me Bs undeservedly. She knew that I got into mischief by talking to my neighbors every time I was excused from class to sit in the back of the room and read!

Mrs. Kipp tried to pass on to us her fascination with the changing of the seasons. At least once a week, during spring, she pointed out the flowers and trees blossoming outside our window. Yet, I didn't share her enthusiasm. At age 13, I was more impressed with Cheryl Anderson blossoming across the aisle from me.

But Mrs. Kipp's greatest impact on me came from my realization that she liked me. That allowed me to like myself more. Her attitude was particularly helpful after my fifth-grade experience. Fifth grade was difficult because my teacher, Miss Hemlock, made clear her belief that children with disabilities did not belong in school. Dad commented that just like Socrates, I had poison hemlock. If I had had my Ph.D. when I entered fifth grade, would she have accepted me?

Mrs. Kipp continued to influence my life long after I left seventh grade. When I visited her just after I turned 34, she told me it was time to think about finding a wife. She may have had some effect; I became engaged the next year. I recalled that she had brought her husband to class to meet us right after she married. Interestingly, she and I married at about the same age. By example, Mrs. Kipp taught me that it was alright for "older people" to wed.

This article was first published in May of 1991 in DLE Update, Sacramento, CA. Reprinted with permission.

My last news of Mrs. Kipp is very sad. She has Alzheimer's disease. Her mind is fading, but her ideas and care continue in the minds and lives of her students.

Chapter Two

Teen Life and Young Adulthood

Being a teenager is stressful, and a disability adds to that stress. Yet my teen years weren't much different from those of my able-bodied peers. The content of this section does not focus on my disability except to describe my positive adaptation to my situation.

Bar Mitzvah

Age 13

Dad's Comments on My Bar Mitzvah

When Bob was 13 years old, he was practicing for his Bar Mitzvah at the Reform Temple of Waterbury. He successfully learned his Torah portion and he succeeded in writing an excellent Bar Mitzvah speech. He was, however, having trouble in doing the oration of the speech. He studied his speech with Mrs. Szanton, his speech therapist, and he practiced it over and over again. What we discovered is that the more thoroughly he learned the speech, the more clearly he delivered it.

When the day came for the Bar Mitzvah, he did such a good job of it that we were all thrilled. He demonstrated to himself and to us that the more thoroughly he knew something, the less his spasticity interfered. In other words, thorough knowledge of what one intends to do also ensures the physiological and physical security of the skills. I suspect that the lesson of corrected practice leads to greater and greater success in performance. Once you learn how to get your act together in one way, you can generalize the lesson to other ways.

Many people came to the Bar Mitzvah who were in the Jewish community, and they were impressed with Bob's performance. Grandma's mother and father came to the Bar Mitzvah, and I wish that my brothers and sister and their spouses and their children could have come.

Bar Mitzvah Speech January 20, 1956

Tonight is different from other Shabbos nights. It is the first time in my life that I can come before you to declare myself your equal. From now on I may perform the rituals of Judaism reserved for adults, such as being part of a minyan (prayer group), making Kiddish (wine blessing), and reading from the Torah. It is a great privilege to have the right to perform these rituals, for in them I will be following the paths of Jews for centuries past. The rituals are a link between me and them. Each time I perform a ritual I will be re-enacting the worship of my ancestors and drawing myself closer to them.

I will be closer to God, too, through my new privileges in the congregation of Israel. I will lean upon Him. Will know God as a friend and guide. My life will be more beautiful and purposeful. All this is now readily available to me by virtue of your granting me the privilege of Bar Mitzvah and the adult status that comes with it.

Bar Mitzvah is an achievement for my parents as well as for me. It is a moment in time when we look back upon years of sacrifice. I want to express my gratitude to my parents for the help they have given me during the years of growth. They have been loving and patient with me under difficult circumstances.

Many others have contributed to my Bar Mitzvah. If it were not for my speech therapist, I would not be able to give this address. If it were not for my physical therapist, I would not be able to stand for this length of time. Many teachers and my rabbi have helped prepare me.

To all of them and to my dear parents especially, I am deeply grateful.

I am grateful to God for the power to be Bar Mitzvah. He gave me a foundation upon which I and many others have built. I worked very hard and I tried to cooperate with those who helped me. But without my own effort there would be no Bar Mitzvah, no Robert Segalman the newly instituted Jew in the congregation of Israel.

Note: My strongest memory of the Bar Mitzvah is that after I read from the Torah, I sat down next to the rabbi. In a loud voice, I said to him, "Nu." In Yiddish, that means, "So, what do you think?" The whole congregation laughed! My grandfather Barney, who claimed to be an atheist, honored me by sitting on the pulpit, wearing a yarmulke, and helping to carry the Torah.

During most of my adult life, I have worshipped as a Friend (unprogrammed Quaker) but I am also very much a Jew.

My dad wrote "Bar Mitzvah." It was in my dad's autobiography, "Letters to My Grandchildren," 2001.

A Real Ham

Age 16

Sometime in the middle of my teenage years (maybe 1959), after I decided that I was too old for Boy Scouts and before I found out that there was an opposite sex, I discovered amateur radio broadcasting. Actually, I discovered short-wave listening first. My friend Louis showed me how to tune our massive and ancient Magnavox radio in the living room. He tuned in the British Broadcasting Corporation (BBC) from London, the Voice of Quito Ecuador, and Radio Moscow.

It wasn't long before I was also listening to the chatter of the radio amateurs, or "hams," and I convinced my parents to buy a good short-wave radio for my bedroom. Most countries license, or simply permit, amateur radio operators to broadcast to each other on special frequencies set aside for them. Thousands of American hams, licensed through examination by the Federal Communications Commission, spend their leisure time talking to each other over the airwaves. Much of their talk is about radio equipment and other hobby information, but hams also provide a free message service for the general public, as well as emergency communications during disasters. With gasoline generators, many hams keep their radios going during earthquakes, hurricanes, and floods, even when normal electrical service is interrupted.

Although Dad protested that I was enough of a ham already, I joined a radio club and attended Friday night meetings. Of course, I could not just spend my time listening to hams; I had

to become one too. Not only did I learn about ham radio there, but the club members introduced me to jelly doughnuts and cigarettes.

The jelly doughnuts I am still addicted to, but my valiant effort to learn to smoke fortunately ended after a few choking episodes. (If I had taken Bill Clinton's advice and not inhaled, I could have avoided the choking.) Mom may have suspected that I had been smoking even when I hadn't, because the club reeked of cigarettes and my clothes smelled of them, too.

Soon after I joined the club, I started studying for my license examination. At that time, the federal "novice" examination required the ability to send and receive Morse code at five words-per-minute and to pass an examination on basic electronics. Actually, it only took me 24 hours to memorize the entire alphabet in Morse code. If I still had that youthful memory, I could keep all of California's crime statistics in my head and be the hero of my unit. I was so impressed with my Morse code ability that I insisted on teaching it to my 8-year-old sister, Ruth. She still teases me about that time I coerced her into spending 20 minutes translating the dots and dashes that I tapped out on the dining room table, only to discover that I had just said: "The refrigerator is cold."

Once I was licensed, I saved up to buy a radio transmitter, so I could talk with other hams (first by Morse code and later by voice). With that done, I spent the rest of my teens lobbying my parents for better and more expensive equipment and antennas. Since I did not drive a car during my teenage years, all my money went into ham gear.

Due to the expense of this equipment and because my ham transmissions interfered with the neighbors' television reception, my hobby did not make me popular. The landlord upstairs stamped his foot in rage when I interfered with his favorite program, "The Honeymooners." I expected him to come downstairs and hit me: "Pow, right in the kisser," Jackie Gleason style.

Television interference wasn't my only equipment problem. I could not afford a motor to rotate my antenna, so I had to go out in the snow to rotate it myself. I had to wear boots. If I ran fast enough to keep warm, I could get by without a coat, as long as my parents were not around to stop me. Astonished at hearing one of those rare female voices on ham radio, I ran out in the snow to rotate the antenna to bring it in clearly. I got back in time to contact her and was truly disappointed to find out that she was an older woman. She was 25!

Ham radio was fun, and it was also a way to escape the emotional strains of being a teenager. Yet, by the time I entered college my interests changed; I have not used my ham radio since. My old equipment with its dusty vacuum tubes is still in the garage, squeezed between my fading school papers and a collection of *Sunset* magazines.

This article was first published in December of 1990 in DLE Update, *Sacramento, CA. Reprinted with permission.*

Old-Time Radio

Age 8 to Adulthood

Many of my fondest childhood memories are of listening to "old-time" radio. Unlike television, radio listening required visualizing what's happening, especially if there was a story line to follow. This mental activity made the listener part of the entertainment process, which is a primary reason that I have a clear memory of so many old radio programs. Perhaps the experience even helped me develop the visualization skills I needed to write. Yet sometimes, visualizing radio events confused me.

For example, readers over 60 may remember Fibber McGee periodically opening his overstuffed closet on Wistful Vista Way and everything coming tumbling out. At age 8, I pictured my Grandmother's hall closet while listening to that program and I was always amazed when I opened her closet and nothing fell out.

Similarly, when radio shows moved to television, my imagination fooled me again. The characters and their environments never looked as attractive on TV as I had pictured them on radio. "Our Miss Brooks," a situation comedy about a high school teacher, starred a young Eve Arden who was much prettier in my radio visualization of her than any actress could possibly be on TV. Some of my recent writing ideas have come from listening to the radio. Garrison Keillor described "Lake Wobegon, Minnesota" on public radio as a "small town where all the women are strong, all the men are good looking, and all the children are above average."

That inspired me to write about "The Berkeley of Wisconsin," the 1960s University of Wisconsin campus, where all the men wore ponytails, the women spouted Karl Marx, and their children chanted, "Power to the People."

One of my favorite radio shows in elementary school was Jack Benny's Christmas Special. During that hour, he visited the employees he had assigned to out-of-the-way places like the musty basements where you could hear the noisy boilers banging. Later, I fantasized about him visiting me in my basement student-office in graduate school. In his penny-pinching manner, he grandly presented me with a used lawnmower blade that he purchased at a yard sale. That fantasy is strange, as I don't remember any yard sales—at least not in my part of the Midwest.

At age 8, I listened to radio broadcasts of the Sioux City Soos baseball, a farm team of the then New York Giants. My family wasn't interested in it, but because of the broadcasts I persuaded Dad to take me to see the Soos play. He must have loved me very much to have sat with me on those hard benches in the 95° heat and humidity watching double-plays and homeruns. Truth be told, he read many science fiction books there while I watched those games. My interest in baseball soon waned and my conception of it became trapped in time back in the 1950s. One of my younger friends who is a baseball enthusiast teases me, because I still think of the A's as being in Philadelphia, the Giants as being in New York, and the Braves as being in Boston.

Over the years, I have enjoyed listening to classical music. Sometimes when I listen, I remember a conversation Dad and I had just before we left Sioux City in 1953. He then looked forward to the availability of classical music on the radio in Waterbury. At the time, I couldn't imagine that the radio would play anything besides popular music, soap operas, and news. I now laugh at my limited concept—at age 9—of what radio could offer.

Just after my 10th birthday, I discovered a soap opera called "Helen Trent," which always began by dramatically asking the question, "Can a woman over 35 still find love and fulfillment?" Because of Helen Trent, I too began to worry when I was unmarried at 35. Unlike Helen, I married at 36 and then moved to Sacramento. Perhaps I had Helen to thank for the inspiration.

This article was first published in January of 1990 in **DLE Update***, Sacramento, CA. Reprinted with permission.*

The Red Brick House
Age 10 to Adulthood

If you stand outside the front door of this office building and look directly across the street and across the empty lot, you will see the back of a red brick house. That house looks very much like my grandparents' Peoria, Illinois home where I spent every summer until I was 19.

Apparently, there were many similar houses built around the country just after the Depression. I wonder how many of them had those marvelous laundry shoots extending from the second floor bathroom all the way to the basement. My favorite pastime was to lure unsuspecting visitors into putting their heads into the first floor shoot on the pretext of telling them something and then dropping a wet wash rag on their heads from the second floor bathroom. (I laughed out loud to my brother's response to this paragraph, which was, "And you wonder why you had so few friends!")

You can see a small second story window on the house across the street, which on our house was replaced by a door and a rickety porch. It was on this porch that my cousin Margaret taught me to kiss when I was 10. That was the same year Grandfather tried to teach me to drive. Unfortunately, the driving wasn't as much fun as the kissing. My spastic legs so limited my control over the foot pedals that Grandfather gave up the first time I almost hit the church next to the parking lot where I was practicing. It was another 15 years before I discovered that I could drive with hand controls, something which I enjoyed until my neck bones began wearing out.

Driving a car wasn't the only form of mobility I tried during my summers in that house. When I was 12, I learned to ride a boy's bicycle with training wheels. The emphasis is on the word "boy's," as my sixth-grade macho image forced me every day to heave my leg over the high rod between the handle bars and the seat rather than more easily mounting Mom's old "girl's" bike, which lay unused in the back of the garage. My bicycling career ended abruptly the next year when I fell off the damn thing and hit my head while I was trying to simultaneously cross a sloping driveway and look at a pretty girl. Grandfather said I needed my brains to make enough money to support him in his old age, and he wasn't about to let me damage them in a cycling accident. He never let me ride a bike again.

Grandfather had strong opinions about nearly everything, or so it seemed to me at age 12, sitting and listening to him in the living room of that red brick house. He liked to sit in his easy chair in his clean, checkered, boxer shorts, and tank-type undershirt, and discuss politics.

In those early days of the Eisenhower Administration, this formerly penniless immigrant would sit in his upper-middle class home a mile from his thriving clothing store and proclaim the evils of capitalism and the glories of socialism. Grandfather's socialism embarrassed me because I confused it with Soviet-style communism. I didn't understand that up until World War II; it was acceptable to be an American socialist.

I liked listening to Grandfather on those lazy summer afternoons, except of course, when my young friends would come to visit. Then my mood would suddenly turn from fascination to embarrassment as he would bid them welcome and return to sipping his high ball and advocating socialism without bothering to don trousers.

So, next time you have had a rough day and you drive by one of those fine old red brick houses, think about your grandfather in his undershorts, smile, and enjoy your evening.

This article was first published (date unknown) in DLE Update, Sacramento, CA. *Reprinted with permission.*

Dating with a Disability
(Or, Where to Find That Special Person)

Dating is an activity that the able-bodied embark upon with little knowledge, less wisdom, and almost no common sense. To complicate such a risky venture with the limitations of a disability can be even more perilous. My experiences with dating prompted me to write advice that may benefit others. Perhaps as a sociologist who spent 20 years as a single adult with a disability, I can suggest some realistic ways for people with disabilities to meet compatible dates.

We all limit the kinds of people we wish to date, and are progressively choosier about who we select for more permanent relationships. One lady I know will date only unmarried men ages 35 to 45, 5'7" to 5'10", who attend weekly church services. In addition, this lady, like everyone else, can only date those men whose own restrictive choices do not exclude her. Each restriction that she or a possible prospective date makes further limits the probability of a successful match.

This probability is further limited by attitudes about a potential date's disability. Everybody (with or without disabilities) limits the kind and degree of disability that they will accept in potential dates. This limits the population of probable dates for people with disabilities. Don't let this scare you. No matter what your disability, there are people more interested in you than in your disability. Your task is to locate them.

To combat such limitations, the potential dater with a disability must locate a greater number than usual of potential dates. It's a "numbers game," and you can increase your odds of success by getting the numbers on your side. There are various methods of locating potential dates.

How you choose to look for dates depends on your personal style of relating and the nature of your disability. There are many places to look. Traditionally, single people gather socially to increase the likelihood of meeting potential dates. The main reason for such gatherings is not to meet potential dates, but for other social reasons. The gathering spot you choose depends on your interests. Religious people attend services and join their congregational singles' club; skiers seek dates on the slopes. Some social opportunities are ongoing, while others are limited to one event.

Some people find dates less formally in grocery stores, laundromats, and at work. One assertive blind friend meets all his dates in the grocery store. He approaches a nice-smelling woman and asks her where to find the milk. While grocery stores and laundromats provide a haphazard and inefficient dating environment, dating people you work with has other risks.

People gather specifically to meet potential dates at singles' bars, but here they have limited opportunity to know someone before having to opt for or decline further intimacy. In college,

I had trouble meeting women that way because my cerebral palsied speech was always more difficult to understand in noisy bars, and I couldn't find a quiet bar within tricycle-distance of campus. Meeting in bars, which has always implied a relaxed sexual morality, became less attractive as I learned about sexually communicable diseases. That option expired altogether with the advent of AIDS.

Video-dating has advantages over the previous two methods: (1) you know more about a person before meeting them; (2) you can decline to meet someone if they do not meet your qualifications based on what you learned from their tape; (3) you can schedule your dates in barrier-free environments (e.g., a deaf lip reader will choose situations in which they can always see their date's lips, and a person who must speak softly will choose quiet places); and (4) describing your disability on videotape permits you to present it anyway you want to, truthfully or not.

Video-dating is probably the only method of meeting women that my friends and I did not try in our single days. At the time, participation cost several hundred dollars—which was beyond our means! Many of these services are still expensive.

Today, with the explosion of the Internet, computer dating has become the mainstay. After completing the computer dating form and clicking on your characteristic choices, you simply peruse for a compatible person. A drawback would be that computer dating services simply provide a list of names and telephone numbers, presenting a surreal situation for many participants. This limitation can be a greater barrier for people with communication disabilities.

My experiences with calls from computer-matched dates who did not understand my CP speech were very frustrating. Computer dating in which the first contact is by mail avoids this problem, but leads to frustration if impaired mobility and/or distance keep the couple apart.

Singles' columns provide barrier-free date matching with the following advantages for people with communication impairments: (1) you can list TTY-relay numbers or mailing addresses; (2) you can present your disability in any way desired (this description eases self-elimination of prospective dates with negative feelings about a particular disability); (3) you can insure your safety and anonymity by listing a post office box and no last name; and (4) special-interest singles' columns, such as those found in a hobby or religious publications, give you added protection and can help find compatible dates.

One friend with severe CP met his wife after she answered his ad. She happens to be able-bodied and answered the ad even though it mentioned his disability because it described characteristics that she had had trouble finding in other men. She met all of his qualifications, some of which he included in the ad. After 17 years together, they are still very much in love.

With so many methods I wonder which will be right for you?

Unpublished, written about 1990.

Dating and the "S" Word

Ages 16 to 65

For me, the greatest problem that resulted from cerebral palsy has been, and to some extent still is, a lack of physical and emotional intimacy. I felt strong sexual urges from puberty on. A psychologist examined me when I was 16, as part of a thorough evaluation of my disability, and commented on my strong interest in sex. He neglected to mention that almost all boys that age have those feelings. I was in an unfair situation. If I had not had CP, that psychologist would not have been examining me. In retrospect, I resent having been told, probably inaccurately, that something was wrong with my sexuality.

My interest was increased by bragging reports from my able-bodied peers who were beginning to date. In retrospect, that psychologist seemed naïve about the nature of 16-year-old boys, and it took me another 10 years to find out that many 16-year-old boys exaggerate their prowess anyway.

Some of my problems with women could have been alleviated had I figured out, or been taught, early on that those women who saw me as their social equal were the women who would see me as most attractive. That information would have been very helpful to me when I was beginning to date. While I had a hunch that that was the case, some verification of that fact from an authority figure would have helped me make better decisions about which women to pursue. Unfortunately, the therapist I was seeing during my college years was not helpful on that score.

Unfortunately, too, the women who find me interesting are usually not the educated, able-bodied women who I find attractive. I seek acceptance as an educated, professionally accomplished, able man despite my disability. Developing a relationship with a woman who is not educated, attractive, and accomplished does not interest me. This lack of congruence between women to whom I was attracted and women who found me attractive led to my being deprived of sex and deeper relationships during much of my adult life.

Marriage

I married in 1978, just after my 36th birthday. My marriage worked well for many years and then stopped working. When my marriage worked, I was happy. During the years that the marriage wasn't working, I was unhappy. A decade of psychotherapy could not resolve that issue. Eventually, I left the relationship. Since then, I have been much more content with life. Sometimes it is less lonely to live alone than to live with someone else.

A very sad part of my marital unhappiness was that I felt that I would betray my wife if I told my parents about our marital problems, and I also feared Dad giving me advice that I might not take. I try to be open with my parents. Communications with them improved enormously after I told them that I was ending my marriage. Now I fly from my home in Sacramento to Los Angeles with a sense of openness and love for my parents. I immensely enjoy my monthly visits. We now get along better than we ever did before.

My wife and I lived together for 28 years. When I moved out, able-bodied friends were incredulous that I left my able-bodied wife. Yet, my friends with disabilities understood my unwillingness to remain, given our growing differences. Deeply religious friends might say that it was God's plan for me to have overwhelming marital problems, as those problems drove me into therapy and the therapy made me a better person.

Media accounts of recent work on the sexual frenzy of insect species attempting to avoid extinction prompt me to mention a similar phenomenon I occasionally notice in adult men with CP. Because I have CP, I have known many other men with that condition. Men with CP, sometimes, appear to have a stronger interest in sex than able-bodied men. I speculate that the possible causes of the phenomenon could be some of the following:

1. Sexual deprivation due to paucity of sexual partners—
   That paucity appears to stem from the following: (a) men with CP have infrequent opportunities to pair with women with disabilities because of low numbers of such women in their vicinity; (b) such men can be physically isolated from available women because of placement in an institution, inability to drive, etc.; or (c) able-bodied women often find such men lacking in looks, economic prospects, and perceived sexual prowess.

2. A need to prove themselves sexually—As such, men lack sexual opportunity, their initial adolescent desires are never fulfilled. Every time sex is unavailable in later life, the adolescent deprivation is relived and the sexual desire increases.

3. Cerebral palsy as a brain dysfunction—As sexual desire originates in the brain, could some kind of brain damage from cerebral palsy enhance such desire?

4. Misinterpretation by the brain—Could the brain misinterpret the brain damage from cerebral palsy as an attempt by nature to create a new species and thus increase the sexual desire in an attempt to perpetuate that new species?

5. A way of passing—Could having regular sex be a way of "passing," just as some light-skinned, successful black people "pass"? I get the feeling from talking to other men with CP that sometimes having regular intimacy gives them a feeling of being able-bodied.

Little is known scientifically about sexual function and sexual emotions among men with CP. Because of the concerns stated above, this is a fertile field for scientific inquiry. I hope that scientists will take up this challenge.

Unpublished, written in 2007.

Chapter Three

College and Graduate School

Ages 18 to 29

I went to college long before any organized accommodations were made for people with disabilities. I was on campus during the turmoil of the 1960s. Perhaps because "change was in the air," my differences from my peers were acceptable. In some ways I was a trailblazer and paved the way for students with disabilities who came after me.

Halls of Cactus

(Alumnus with a Disability Looks Back) Ages 18 to 22

In September 1961, 10 months after JFK's election, I became the second student with multiple disabilities at what was then called Texas Western College (TWC). Back then, I could walk, albeit with an awkward cerebral-palsied gait, which made college life easier in a time before wheelchair accessible campuses.

Although I had been accepted at what I snobbishly considered a prestigious eastern college, my parents insisted that I attend TWC when Dad began working in El Paso. Reluctantly, I left Connecticut's lovely Naugatuck Valley, where we had lived since I was 10, for this unknown place in the desert. Yet, I was enticed by the promise of snowless winters and coeds wearing shorts in March.

The Dormitory

Another enticement was my parents' promise that I could live in a dormitory. With sudden unexpected trepidation, I moved into the dormitory on Labor Day. Later that day, I bought a freshman beanie and joined other freshmen in the traditional painting of the college insignia on a nearby mountainside. The same weekend I met my good friend, Billy Best, now a retired probation officer in Santa Cruz.

The only problem with dormitory life was my vanity in not asking for a chair to sit on in the shower. My perilous barefoot balance necessitated such concentration to remain upright under the unpredictable spray that I did not always get completely clean. During sophomore year, a student on crutches put a chair in the shower, but I was too vain to ask to use it. The elderly dorm mother, reflecting the values of many people at that time, had proclaimed that people who are disabled should not attend college, so I would not ask her help.

Two dormitory neighbors made homebrew in their room, but I only drank the stuff when I could not decline gracefully. It tasted awful, and there was no point in drinking it when Juarez, Mexico, was only five miles away. There we could buy mixed drinks for 25 cents apiece, while we contemplated the demise of our virginity for an additional $2.50.

Even if I was too shy to participate in dormitory pranks, I still took special delight in each event. I did help several friends plan the capture of the alligator who resided in a pool in the city plaza. They dumped it in the campus swimming pool where it supposedly nipped a coed skinny dipping in the moonlight.

Another memory is of the only two bearded fellows in our dormitory. One night they drank too much and began fighting. Later, one of them returned to the dorm, looked at his reflection in the cigarette machine mirror, and put his fist through it. I wondered if, perhaps, that man was not attempting to hit the other drunk man, but was angry at himself.

Classes and Grades

Before classes began, I obtained permission to type all exams and in-class themes in the Dean of Men's Office, because I write very slowly and almost illegibly. Yet on the first day of class, the English professor did not know of this arrangement, so my first theme was handwritten and came back with a humiliating "C."

Throughout college I worried about getting the grades I would need to enter graduate school. By taking only 12 credits each semester and easy summer school courses, I had time to concentrate on difficult classes during the long semesters. To keep my grades up, I avoided a few difficult courses such as chemistry and Elizabethan literature. I can't quote Macbeth, and I don't know the chemical composition of sugar, but I did get into graduate school. My greatest college trauma was failing calculus, which was then the flunk-out course for engineers.

Even though 50% of the class failed and I was the only nonengineer in the class, I was never consoled.

Coeds

Eating our meals in the coed dining room was a primary attraction of dorm life. The prospect of watching lovely creatures slither between tables brought me to many meals. The exertion of walking a block from the dormitory to the dining room was well worth the effort. Those were the days before the sexual revolution, but discussions of necking and petting brought as much attention as spicier discussions do today.

Those were sexually repressed days and once when a young lady came to dinner in a strapless dress, I could think of nothing else for days. Generally, such thoughts only occupied my adolescent mind 80% of the time.

One way to meet women was by hitchhiking to class. (I was 30 before I learned to drive a car.) People came to know me and often stopped. If a coed gave me a ride more than once and was not wearing a wedding or engagement ring, I thought about asking her out. I was rarely that bold, but I thought about it a lot.

My Job

During my junior and senior years, I worked on the student committee which arranged lectures, dances, and art exhibits. This was my first exposure to bureaucracy and provided an introduction to brainstorming. During one meeting, we were searching for themes that might attract cultured Eastern students and faculty. I introduced a variation of the concept of "Halls of Ivy" and spent a half-hour explaining the virtues of a recruiting campaign based on the theme "Halls of Cactus"; that monologue was the precursor to many arguments that I made before bureaucratics throughout my career. The two deans for whom I worked were unusually patient teachers.

My makeshift office in a basement storage room next to the bowling alley had advantages. I learned to recognize the number of pins knocked down from the sound, and my Student Union Building key permitted my friends and me to indulge in occasional nocturnal ping-pong games.

Conclusion

The deans, student activities staff, faculty, and students all took an interest in me. Several professors spent long hours advising me on a research project that was published in a scientific journal. At TWC I was a big fish in a small pond and received encouragement and assistance unavailable at most universities. That support system was probably more effective than any provided today by the most sophisticated disabled student services office; it enhanced my college years.

Several years after I graduated, Texas Western College became the University of Texas at El Paso, and that is where I tell people I went to college. After all, why shouldn't I benefit from the college's increased prestige?

This article was first published in June of 1987 in NOVA, *the alumni magazine at the University of Texas at El Paso; then republished in August of 1991 in* DLE Update, *Sacramento, CA. Reprinted with permission.*

The Tallahassee Decision

Ages 22 to 23

We were talking about class reunions over coffee a while back. After a colleague, Alexander Abernathy, told a story about a beautiful woman he met at his high school reunion in San Luis Obispo, it was my turn. I started to tell him about a gorgeous Southern lady I met during my years at Florida State University (FSU), Tallahassee in 1966. But just as my mind was weaving a tale of unbelievable romantic adventure, Alexander spoiled my story by asking the inevitable question, "Why Tallahassee?"

Actually, I debated for some time whether to go to FSU, because I had also been offered a scholarship at the University of California, Santa Barbara (UCSB). My parents wanted me to go to UCSB because it was closer to their home in El Paso, Texas, had a better graduate program, a milder climate, and had offered a better scholarship. When they realized I was leaning toward Florida State, they offered to fly me to both campuses to have a look around before making a final decision. But in my adolescent confusion, I was adamant and did not want to be swayed by facts. I chose Tallahassee because it was so far away, and my parents preferred Santa Barbara! Frustrated, Mom said, "How can you go to Tallahassee? You can't even say it!" I hope that I have matured since that time. I was 22 years old and had little on my mind besides accumulating college degrees and chasing women.

Although I had brains, I had very little sense, which explains why I was more successful with degrees than with women. I pursued women as if they were term papers, and compulsively said the same stock things to each of them as if I were inserting the romantic equivalent of footnotes. I had both the romantic drive and skill of the Woody Allen character. No wonder I met with the same lack of success.

In spite of this immaturity, I had a strong value system. I might not have chosen Florida State had I known in advance the university's strange attitude towards blacks. Although my African roommate with chocolate skin openly attended classes and dated Caucasian co-eds, American blacks were excluded. They could only enroll in the all-black university across town. In fact, the decision to attend Florida State was a good one because of what I learned about the ironies of Southern racial practices. One friend suspected that I must have been there just as Jim Crow was overturned and civil rights were instated. I did not see changes happening around me.

Florida State's enrollment policy reminded me of my friend Alan's behavior when we were partners in Monopoly games in grade school. Alan really liked the color red and would only play with the red houses. He never won because there weren't enough red houses. Even after I painted some other houses red with Mom's fingernail polish, Alan would only play with the original red ones. Alan's attitude toward red was as illogical as the university's toward blacks.

Fortunately, the university's attitude and Alan's have both matured. The university now admits students of all races, and Alan is a successful realtor selling houses of all colors.

This article was first published in March of 1989 in DLE Update, *Sacramento, CA. Reprinted with permission.*

Getting a Ph.D.
Ages 23 to 29

Yesterday, on Bay Area Rapid Transit (BART), a very pretty woman who has a master's degree in social work and uses a wheelchair chatted with me and spoke of going on for a doctorate. If you have read other chapters of this book, you know that I cannot resist a request from a woman, especially a pretty and intelligent woman.

Thus, when she asked about my experience in the Ph.D. program (1966–1972), I remembered that this book needs a chapter describing my University of Wisconsin–Madison (UW) days. So, Beth Smith, Licensed Clinical Social Worker, from the Richmond Bound BART train: Here is the rest of the answer to your question. Here are the things that I didn't have time to tell you with my voice-output computer (AAC device) between the Powell Street and Berkeley Stations.

Why UW–Madison?

My choice to do my Ph.D. at the University of Wisconsin–Madison was a simple one. UW–Madison was the highest ranking of the universities that accepted me into its doctoral program and offered me financial aid. My late-adolescent brain was tempted by an offer from the University of Utah by what I misunderstood at the time to be the Mormon polygamous lifestyle; but no, common sense prevailed.

I remember my bus ride into Madison that early autumn day in 1966. The greenery pleased me and resembled the countryside around Florida State University in Tallahassee where I had just finished a master's degree. How naive I was in thinking that I was just embarking on an academic experience.

Little did I know how much the influence of the Vietnam War and the development of the women's movement and the black student movement on campus would influence my thinking and how I would lead the rest of my life. While creating positive social change had always been a focus for me because of Dad's values and activities, the values of students and faculty in Madison then made creating positive social change an even stronger life focus for me than it had been before. The values that I learned in Madison and the role models I met there (who approached life with such intensity) strongly influenced my efforts to create the national Speech-to-Speech service. They taught me that life is best when led with enormous passion. (It was only later that I learned how messy passion is.)

Problems with Winter

Just as Mrs. Kipp, my sixth-grade teacher, taught us that Napoleon's great enemies in Russia were General Cold, General Snow, and General Mud; similarly, my greatest challenge in Madison was winter weather. The sheer size and hilly nature of the Madison campus made me reliant on an electric golf cart, while at the smaller campuses at Florida State University, Tallahassee, and University of Texas, El Paso, I had walked and hitchhiked from class to class. Relying on a golf cart, and later on a tricycle, may have deprived me of exercise and led to the deterioration of my ambulation ability during those years. That deterioration was also promoted by the effect of cold on my body. After a few months of cold weather, my legs ached terribly whenever I walked.

Besides winter weather, another great obstacle to successful life in Madison was the inexperience of my physicians (and probably most physicians then and to some extent even now) in treating people with muscle disorders who have lifestyles that require very high cognitive functioning. Here's what happened.

Problems with Medication

When I finished my master's in Tallahassee in August 1966, I visited my family in El Paso before leaving for Madison and checked in with my neurologist. For reasons I don't know, he took me off Elavil, the medication that controlled my depression. Thus, six weeks into my Ph.D. studies, I became very depressed. Fortunately, I had the sense to explain to the treating psychiatrist that I had done well on Elavil. He put me back on Elavil, and within a week I was out of the hospital, attending classes, and functioning well. I could tell that on Elavil I was slightly paranoid and not as bright as I could be. In retrospect, my ability to do advanced statistics was significantly diminished and I was slightly suspicious of other people. Unfortunately, it was another 15 years before we realized that these problems were attributable to the side effects of Elavil.

The problem resulting from my being "off" Elavil brought my medical problem to the attention of a neurology professor at the medical school, and it had an interesting outcome (in retrospect). At that time, several new drugs became available to treat CP muscle tension, and this professor convinced me to try them. Several weeks later, I began having problems keeping up with my academic work and staying awake in class. I made no connection between my academic problems and my medication and struggled along for some time, barely getting my work completed and always being exhausted. Sadly, he kept me on those drugs for a whole year.

Fortunately, the next December, I had stayed on campus over Christmas to study and came down with pneumonia. I say fortunately, because my cousin, who was a physician in Madison, came to check on me. He saw the filthy living conditions in the co-op where I lived and convinced me to return home to Texas. He, in fact, spent two hours cleaning (with a torn UW T-shirt) all the dirty dishes that the 18 of us had allowed to accumulate in the main sink of our co-op over Christmas vacation. Back in Texas, Mom helped me regain my health in a much cleaner environment. Now, the other fortunate thing about my return to Texas was that Mom noticed how much medicine I was taking. She suspected that the medication was causing my academic problems. I saw a local physician right away who took me off everything but Elavil, and many of my academic problems disappeared. (Elavil made graduate school more difficult, but not impossible.)

Academics

As long as I wasn't having medication problems, the doctoral curriculum was no more difficult than my master's or upper-level undergraduate curriculum. The only course that was difficult was statistics. I had more trouble understanding statistics in the master's and Ph.D. programs than I did as an undergraduate, even though the material was similar. I suspect that problem related to the cognitive side effects of Elavil, which were milder than the other drugs that my Madison neurologist had me try.

Co-op Living

For almost all my time at UW, I lived in a large, three-story house with 17 other students, some of whom are still my friends. Men lived on one floor and women on another. This was my first experience living in the same house with women other than my mother and my sister. In some ways, it prepared me for marriage.

In Quaker tradition, our house was run on consensus. That is, we all had to come to unity on community decisions before taking action. Consensus can be long and tedious. Reaching unity on whether to have the cat fixed or have a Christmas tree led to endless discussions, some of which were humorous.

My Introduction to Quakers

It was through the Friends Campus Center that I was introduced to a religion that I have practiced for many years. The center was organized by the Madison Society of Friends (also called Quakers), a small, liberal, Protestant religious group. Unprogrammed Friends Meetings (as opposed to Programmed Friends Churches) are places for silent worship. Unprogrammed Friends worship God and fight for social justice and an end to both war and capital punishment.

As a humorous aside about our abhorrence of capital punishment: once, later in life, before rise from worship, I mentioned to the congregation my sadness over the execution of Saddam Hussein. A friend responded jokingly, "You can sure tell that this is a Quaker Meeting, after that remark."

I see no conflict between being a Quaker and being a Jew. Our beliefs are similar. I worship as a Jew when I visit my parents and my brother and enjoy that worship as I do my visits to the Sacramento Friends Meeting where I am a member. Friends appear to be better listeners than Jews.

Conclusion

Getting a Ph.D. was a vital step toward my success as a person with a severe, multiple disability. The sign on the back of my wheelchair that says: "Bob Segalman, Ph.D., SC.D. (Hon.), America's only known citizen with cerebral palsy to hold two doctorates," sure makes the public treat me better. Most of my jobs only required a master's degree; yet, without a Ph.D., I doubt that I would have been hired. OK, Beth Smith, LCSW, did I answer your question?

Unpublished, written in 2007.

Talking by Numbers
Ages 23 to 25

Every time we go through a reorganization of one kind or another at work to increase efficiency, I remember one master of business administration student's attempt to increase efficiency in our graduate school boardinghouse at the University of Wisconsin (1966–1972). Vernon Verbal specialized in time-and-motion studies, and he knew that the 18 of us wasted a lot of time repeating ourselves. We each had our pet comments that we used again and again, especially when a person of the opposite sex waltzed by or something else happened to prevent us from thinking.

To rectify the situation, Vernon took our 99 most common expressions and gave them each a number. He asked us all to memorize the 99 expressions and their numbers so we could communicate just by calling out the numbers. He was truly an optimist. Can you imagine a bunch of college students memorizing all that just to humor a crazy, compulsive Vernon?

Recently, I came across this list of expressions and remembered how many things seemed important on campus in the 1960s that are of little consequence now. Although I had to omit the juicier expressions, the ones listed below truly reflect the times. I've included the original numbers assigned each comment just in case you want to improve your communication!

Many political comments were typical of the time and place. One left-of-center fellow responded to all remarks he disagreed with on any topic from feeding the cat to doing his homework with, "that's a capitalistic attitude." #63. Each time the telephone rang, he pointed to it imitating a Nixon pose and accent saying, "this phone is tapped." #21.

Another political (and gastronomic) observer used to watch me filling my plate and say, "the helping you're taking now is bigger than LBJ's budget." #87. What LBJ's budget had to do with my appetite I never figured out, but everything was supposed to have political connotations in those days. Current events also taught us that we could win arguments by claiming that our opponent had a "credibility gap." #13.

In Wisconsin, the greatest insult that liberal students could cast was, "'that fellow must be related to Senator Joseph McCarthy." #39.

One housemate's favorite response to any off-the-wall remark was, "your draft board would not like to hear you say that." #97.

Several women had sayings combining the openness of the times with traditional goals. For example, Henrietta, the petite tuba player who lived upstairs, would often whine, "I want to get married." #56. She said this as a general expression of woe to no one in particular at least once a day. She finally married a super macho piccolo player, and they've made beautiful music together for 20 years. Another less traditional woman loved to run through the halls early in the morning awakening everyone with the cry, "pregnancy is the opiate of women." #29.

A third co-ed liked to respond, "don't be sexist!" (#65) to any remark she disagreed with on any topic. No wonder everyone, even other liberal women, avoided her!

We used several comments repeatedly to avoid work around the house. My favorite was, "I have a dissertation to write." #55. Another frequent comment along the same line was, "but I cleaned my room last year." #42.

Several of us who were social science majors came up with phrases which we used repeatedly, "that's a value judgment," (#76), and "I question the validity of your data," (#88). These were classroom arguments that worked equally well in boardinghouse bull sessions. Our housemates sometimes even bought our arguments when we had no idea what we were talking about.

Vernon's system never worked at the boardinghouse, but perhaps it will work on my job. It really could shorten meetings for us. All we'd have to do is go through the minutes of every committee that has met for the last 10 years. We would then number all proposals and all responses, and when they come up again, we could refer to them by number to make things more efficient. Maybe this suggestion will earn me a merit award, even though my idea several months back about edible lottery tickets didn't.

This article was first published (unknown date) in DLE Update, *Sacramento, CA. Reprinted with permission.*

That Big House
Ages 23 to 29

At lunch break, one of the older managers was telling us how exciting his life was in a college dorm and asked me what my college living arrangements had been. I said that by the time I entered graduate school, men and women were living together. His face lit up and his pupils expanded until I explained that it was an experiment set up by a religious group.

In 1966 at the University of Wisconsin, the local Quaker Meeting established a co-education living center. This was a daring step in 1966 when universities still tried to control their students' glands. The meeting rented a defunct rooming house just off campus with living facilities on the first floor, bedrooms for men on the second floor, and bedrooms for women on the third floor. This floor arrangement reflected the theory that women had more self-control and could pass the men's floor on the way to their own without yielding to temptation.

The Quakers recruited residents from a wide range of backgrounds and were reported to have had long arguments over whether I was their token disabled person or token Southerner. (Nomads are identified by their last abode, and I had spent the previous year sweating out a master's in Tallahassee—pun intended.)

As housemates, our biggest challenge was to govern ourselves by the Quaker rules of consensus. Everyone in the house had to agree on any major issue before action was taken. Although such a system worked fine for Quaker congregations, getting 18 argumentative graduate students to agree on fixing the cat or taking out the garbage was a bigger challenge.

I received an unrequested, but thorough, education on the reproductive rights of cats and the imperialistic implications of garbage collection. The cat, I did not care about, but somehow I always got stuck with garbage duty, and still do.

We also disagreed intensely on housekeeping standards. For example, one mathematics doctoral student had such a strong cognitive sense of order that he never felt a need to clean his room or anything else. Unfortunately, he roomed with a vocal and demanding accounting major who kept his possessions in orderly rows just like his figures. In that house, my meager arbitration skills were tested and found wanting.

As is common among college students, some of us were very idealistic. Part of our idealism was reflected in our willingness to provide overnight housing for the homeless ex-students who wandered many campuses in the late 1960s. The rescue missions often called late at night requesting floor space for transients. It became such a regular ritual that one quiet night after a few too many beers, I called the mission to ask, "don't you like us any more? How come you haven't sent us any transients?"

In conclusion, something was bound to happen when all those young people with explosive glands moved in together. Five couples married during my five years in the house. The most creative suitor had taken his love for a walk past a junk yard where she had admired an ornate bathtub on top of the heap. She arrived home the next day after class to find that very bathtub taking up most of her tiny, third-floor bedroom as a token of his affection. That bathtub contained the engagement ring. Three guys had spent three hours dragging it up there. That couple just celebrated their 20th anniversary.

This article was first published in December of 1987 in DLE Update, *Sacramento, CA. Reprinted with permission.*

The Colored Oleo Caper

Ages 23 to 29

I was loping down the right lane of Highway 50 the other morning, hoping to get to work without being rear-ended, when a strange thought came to me. It struck me that even with a criminology background and seven years as a criminal justice researcher, I still have no personal experience in crime. You guessed it, like millions of other sheltered Americans, I have never committed an illegal act (except for stealing hub caps). Well now, let's think about that a moment. Oh yes, there is something—right, the colored oleo caper!

I was 25 that year (1968), and one of my weekly chores in our boarding house was to color the oleo. Wisconsin law forbade the sale of yellow oleo. We had to buy this yucky looking white oleo and mix in a gooey, yellow dye that always streaked, producing putrid yellow stuff that was supposed to look like butter. After weeks of nasty dinner table remarks about my oleo mixing abilities, I was determined to find an alternative to that striped junk.

We were discussing the oleo problem one night over three-day-old spaghetti and last week's tuna fish when Husani Durabi suggested we bootleg oleo. (Husani was an economics Ph.D. candidate from Pakistan who later dropped out to work for "our" government. He became Adviser on Ethics to Spiro Agnew three days before Agnew pled nolo contendere.) The year before, Husani had lived in another boarding house where they brought in a station wagon full of the "yellow stuff" from the Wisconsin border town of Rockford, Illinois, every other month.

Many of my housemates wanted no part of this scheme. They planned government careers and feared that something might get into their records, but four of us were game.

As a result, the four of us became repeat criminal offenders: Pete Wrong became a demography professor; Helen Louise

Night teaches second grade; and Russ Guest now practices psychiatry in Michigan (last I heard, it was so cold where Russ works that he spends all his time thawing egos); and me. We were in Pete's old station wagon, the one with overdrive. I remember that part because once Pete almost took a toll collector's hand off trying to save gas by going through the toll booth in overdrive. It was a good hour's drive to Rockford but the time passed quickly. Pete, with a straight face, spent the hour proving that with current demography training programs, by the year 2000 there would be more demographers in the US than people.

Buying butter was out of the question. Do you know how much it cost in Wisconsin in 1968 to buy enough butter to feed 19 college students three meals a day? Dairy prices were always high. The dairy lobby did its share of "milking," and it always "buttered" up the legislature and skimmed off the "cream." Besides that, I was not going to discuss anything with the coed in the room above me who did the buying. She was a Trotskyite and I could not talk with her without getting a half-hour lecture on the evils of capitalism or the immorality of bathing (which denied fish ample access to the water supply). Besides that, she stunk. This was 1967 and smelling awful was the "in" thing. As we approached Rockford that first Sunday afternoon, I was amazed by the sudden increase in traffic. There were cars everywhere, mostly big sedans and station wagons. Empty cars headed into the city, and full ones headed out. The grocery store parking lot where we stopped was packed with people hauling out cartons of the stuff. Leaving the city I saw returning Wisconsinites, mostly teenagers, leaning out of the backs of station wagons making sure their precious yellow cargo did not fall out. We saw some police cars as we crossed back into Wisconsin, but not enough of them to stop very many violators. Perhaps they could stop every fifteenth car. The police could no more keep colored oleo out of Wisconsin than they could keep ants out of a picnic. Many of us speculated about what the state police did with confiscated oleo.

Pete Holmes, who later became an expert on the speed of falling water droplets, told us a story that came from a very drunk activist from Students for a Democratic Society (SDS)*. He was convinced that the state police kept all confiscated oleo frozen until the next student protest so the university police could boil it and pour it on the sidewalks for the demonstrators to slip in!

Some readers will spot an inconsistency between my jokes in this chapter about "my criminal history," and my comments elsewhere in the book that I didn't want to do anything during those years to compromise my eligibility for a security clearance later in life. (Just remember, I am only joking about a "criminal history.")

There is one good outcome to this. On the next "Administrator I" exam, if they ask me why I have worked in so few areas of the department, I can say that my criminal history prevented me from getting a security clearance outside crime statistics.

*Students for a Democratic Society, an organization against the war in Vietnam. (SDS was also referred to as the best dating club on campus.)

This article was published in July of 1987 in DLE Update, Sacramento, CA. Reprinted with permission.

War Stories
Ages 23 to 29

To the dismay of my activist friends on campus, on both sides of the Vietnam War issue, I spent most of the war completing my degree. I was determined to complete my 200-page thesis no matter who was being tear-gassed. My friends never understood how I could spend 10 hours a day writing. Of course, my mind was on graduation, leaving the Midwest winters, and buying a California house with a 7% mortgage. Perhaps I was the original Yuppie.

In true Yuppie fashion, I was less afraid of being injured than of being arrested. My real fear was of somehow losing my eligibility for the federal security clearance that I might need someday. During the now famous demonstration against Dow Chemical Company recruiting on campus, I hid in a faculty lounge with some older professors. Meanwhile, the younger faculty and a few graduate students donned WW II gas masks and ran back and forth to the demonstration bringing us reports.

The closest I came to any kind of rebellious activity was riding my large tricycle the wrong way down a special lane reserved for busses. I wanted to shorten my travel time enabling me to get to class in winter before my beard froze. I stopped using that lane after my first encounter with a big city bus going the other way. The driver stopped the bus and waited for me to get out of the way, but just seeing that huge thing looming down at me quashed my rebellious spirit.

I did come close to being a victim of antiwar activity once when my graduate student office was tear-gassed. That office was in the basement of the Baptist Women's Dormitory squeezed between a Coke machine and drying underwear.

During a student riot, a tear gas bomb was inadvertently lobbed into the basement window. Fortunately, I was out chasing a coed at the time, so my basic instincts saved me from asphyxiation. The only aftereffect was the lingering smell of tear gas in my books. A year later, I sat in my Los Angeles office, opened a book, nostalgically smelled the tear gas, and remembered more exciting days. Similarly, one of my friends here at work, who lived through those days, recently signed up for our department's training course in tear gas use just because the smell brought back such pleasant memories.

Another tear-gassing had its bright side. One friend was undergoing a rigorous Ph.D. oral examination when, halfway through the grilling, the overwhelming odor of tear gas poured into the room and interrupted the interrogation. After relocating to another room, the examiners lost their sadistic enthusiasm and granted my friend his degree.

The other great thing about tear gas was the smell it gave your clothes. The ideal ploy was to return to our boardinghouse from a student demonstration smelling of tear gas. Having to strip down to your skivvies before going in the door was the ultimate status symbol.

My best war story is about my then roommate, Howard, who was called up by the National Guard. One of Howard's professors asked why he had missed several classes only to receive the smart aleck response that my friend was in full dress riot gear assigned to guard the water fountain in the law library. The professor, an outspoken elderly woman with a pronounced southern drawl, responded with a cluck, "My goodness gracious! That water fountain needs military protection about as much as my pet turtle." Well, that's as exciting as my war stories get. Do you other "baby boomers" have something to contribute? Guest columns are always welcome.

This article was published in (date unknown) in DLE Update, *Sacramento, CA. Reprinted with permission.*

What Do You Want to Be When You Grow Up?

About Age 46

Part of education is choosing a career, and that is the subject of this piece. It used to be that people would go off to a desert island to meditate and decide on their life's work, but our department has a simpler solution.

Career Day

Every year, our department has Career Day so we can all choose interesting careers; if not first careers, then second careers. The program includes classes such as one on resume writing and one on job interviews. Did you know that one way to get over the jitters in a job interview is to try imagining all the panel members as they were five hours previously? For example, they may have been eating breakfast in their skivvies. The program also included classes on job relationships and networking opportunities. I have always thought those were fancy words for apple polishing and making constructive use of gossip.

Career Day gave me all kinds of ideas about second careers. I'd like to try something different next time around. Now that people are living so long, many of us may have a chance for a second career.

Second Careers

I would like to be a physician in my second career. They make more money than a Ph.D., and anybody else for that matter. Besides that, everyone waits on them and calls them "doctor." Car sales persons and telephone solicitors are the only people who call me doctor. (Not that I like to be called doctor all the time, it makes me feel too distant, but once a month is a nice ego boost.) If I become a physician, maybe I will be a psychiatrist so people will tell me lurid stories.

One of my "shrink" friends says that she wants to be a dentist next time around so she can put lots of instruments in people's mouths to shut them up. She'd also like to be a dentist because so few people argue with them. Who knows, maybe she'll end up in psychiatric dentistry studying people's teeth to learn more about their emotions, or in dental psychiatry studying people's emotions to learn more about their teeth.

Some people chose second careers in hopes of solving their personal problems. A good buddy of mine began a master's program in marriage counseling to improve the chances of saving his fourth marriage. Not only did he become an excellent marriage counselor, but to everyone's surprise, his professor became his fifth wife!

One colleague said that in her next career she wants to be a Disclosure Officer for the IRS. Those folks devote their time to telling people why the IRS won't release people's tax files. As one of them said, he has 99,000 ways to say "no" and spends most of his time doing that. A sadist's delight!

One co-worker, in contrast, seems more interested in power than money. She wants to be a big rig truck driver next time so people will quit pushing her around. She's enthralled with the power to push all those little cars off the road.

My dad, incidentally, was lucky enough to have a second career and revenge at the same time. After 25 years as an overburdened social worker, he became a sociology professor who wrote books blasting inadequate social service programs.

In summary, Career Day was fun and educational. It gave many people concrete ideas on how to proceed with their careers, and it gave me great fantasies.

This article was first published in August of 1988 in DLE Update, *Sacramento, CA. Reprinted with permission.*

Chapter Four

Work

Ages 29 to 61

I was one of the first people with a significant disability to work full-time for the State of California for 30 years. During those years, I made a contribution, and had some fun. Few people with severe cerebral palsy are privileged to enjoy long-time careers in a professional capacity. I was one of the lucky ones. I was employed first as a social worker, then as a crime statistician, and finally as a rehabilitation researcher. During a two-year leave of absence from my last major employment, I was the lead statewide outreach person for telephone access for people with speech disabilities, a job classification that I invented.

In retirement, I work almost full-time as the volunteer CEO of Speech Communications Assistance by Telephone, Inc., a 501c3 that promotes Speech-to-Speech and other telephone access services for people with speech disabilities.

How Much Education Compensates for How Much Disability?

Age 29

I became a California state employee in the early 1970s. It was close to the time that McGovern selected Eagleton, and Nixon encountered Watergate. However, I'm still working for the same employer which is more than you can say for either of them! Finding employment was particularly difficult for someone with a visible disability before legislation outlawing discrimination in disability hiring. I had cerebral palsy from birth; at that time, I used a cane, spoke with slurred speech, and sometimes drooled.

The Initial Screening

By the time I found a job, I had sent out 300 resumes over six months, and that was before professional people began having trouble finding state jobs. I first visited the California State Personnel Board (SPB) to begin a complex process of applying for many state jobs some of which required both written and oral examinations. Obtaining a state job is less complicated now than it was several decades ago. For many types of entry-level jobs, state offices can directly hire persons with visual, hearing, speech, physical, or developmental disabilities.

Even after all my efforts, the odds were probably still against me as unemployment levels among people with disabilities has always been atrociously high, and my problems speaking to potential employers by telephone worsened those odds. I placed calls myself to assure callers of my telephone capability, yet many employers lost interest after 20 seconds of listening to me speak.

Unusual Bait

The supervisor who finally hired me was pleased to lure a Ph.D. into a state job which only required a master's. My doctorate appeared to compensate for the disability. Jokingly I wondered what the exchange values were in this process. How much education compensates for how much of a disability? Had I held an MD but been blind and deaf, would I still have been offered that same master's level job (if accommodations enabled me to do the work required)? Other people with disabilities tell me of success obtaining employment because of being unusually overqualified. Such tactics are not new. Physicians immigrating to this country often take jobs as lab technicians upon arrival, while immigrant lawyers become law clerks.

A Job I Could Do

My first job was as a social worker in a hospital for people with developmental disabilities. The staff worked in teams, and fortunately there was a vacancy for a team member with writing skills. My colleagues interviewed the clients and their families while I wrote case reports, interview summaries, and correspondence. I was so pleased to be employed that I did not mind the work or being unable to use my Ph.D. research skills. Most staff members preferred interviewing to written work, so the arrangement was satisfactory for most of my years at the hospital. By the fourth staff reorganization seven years later, however, there were not enough counselors to divide the work into oral and written tasks, so I transferred out of the hospital into a research job.

Like everyone else in a first job, I made my share of mistakes. When anyone parked illegally in disabled parking, I took great joy blocking them in with my car and wandering off. I particularly enjoyed doing this to physicians because they were coddled by everyone especially the hospital administrator.

Accommodations

In addition to restructuring my job to limit oral tasks, my employer provided an electric typewriter to substitute for my poor handwriting and a telephone amplifier for my whispered speech. My colleagues eventually introduced me to most of the hospital staff in order to prevent them from mistaking me for one of the adult clients with cerebral palsy. As with ethnic minorities, people frequently have trouble telling us apart.

Many people with cerebral palsy who walk with an awkward gait and talk with whispered speech are also mentally challenged, even though many of them are not. Because the temptation to stereotype all people with cerebral palsy at the hospital as mentally challenged patients was strong, the staff had trouble viewing me as a professional person. My first day on the job, I was asked to leave the employee credit union because the staff believed that I was a client who had wandered in and not an employee trying to open an account.

My Special Efforts

In addition to accommodations made by the employer, I also had to make accommodations. Employees with disabilities often value their jobs more and exert extra effort to do a good job. They have difficulty finding jobs and try hard to keep the ones they have. Most of them have especially good work and attendance habits. I was the only social worker wearing a white shirt and tie every day; that reinforced my professional image and differentiated me from the clients.

Every chance I could I used vacation time when I was sick in an attempt to keep a good sick leave record. Call it paranoia—maybe? Perhaps, however, some people with disabilities have a healthy kind of anxiety about their jobs that make them better workers. They may feel that they do not have the option to goof off as some other workers do.

When I took the job, I even thought of shaving my beard to improve my appearance. Yet arriving at work each day with a scratched face (resulting from a spastic hand manipulating an electric razor) seemed less desirable than arriving with a well-trimmed beard.

An Unusual Opportunity

My most rewarding work at the hospital concerned an 8-year-old girl diagnosed with cerebral palsy and cognitive disabilities, who I will call "Debbie." She had been placed in a sign language class because some children with intellectual challenges learn to communicate with a few basic signs. When Debbie learned to sign unusually easily, a psychologist tested her intelligence using sign language and discovered that it was normal. Because she could not speak, Debbie had been misdiagnosed as "cognitively impaired." After learning to sign, Debbie learned self-help skills allowing her family to take her home to live. I taught Debbie and her family some of the tricks for living with cerebral palsy. As a role model, I gave them hope for her future.

Conclusion

Although recent years have been more professionally rewarding with more interesting assignments, more articles published, and higher salary, I don't regret those years as a hospital social worker. After the hectic years of graduate school, I was delighted to have evenings and weekends free. The free time enabled me to marry, learn to drive a car, and buy my first house. I did well as a Ph.D. in a job requiring only a master's degree, just as I did well as the smartest child in my slow-moving class. (Added in 2008: I now have similar advantages as the youngest person in my senior high-rise apartment building.)

This article was first published in (date unknown) in DLE Update, *Sacramento, CA; then republished in April of 1988 in* Mainstream Magazine, *San Diego, CA. Reprinted with permission.*

Vroom! Vroom!

Guess What, Mom?

About Age 31

Because I have cerebral palsy (CP) and have always had trouble controlling many of my body movements, it was

assumed by the adults around me that I would never be able to drive a car. My parents never discussed the possibility, but in high school I did convince my daredevil grandfather to take me out for a driving lesson. During the first 10 minutes of that lesson, I almost ran into a church in the parking lot where I was attempting to navigate. Further evidence of my inability to control moving objects of which I had charge came when I tried to ride a horse. The horse passed under a low tree branch as I slowly slid off his back and landed on my behind.

After that, through college and graduate school, I made no further attempts to drive a car. I did ride a tricycle and a power golf cart. I lived in Wisconsin and during winter, the cart's accelerator would freeze up while driving, making it impossible to stop without heading for the nearest snow bank. One cold Saturday night I was on the way home from a movie with my date riding on the back of the cart when the accelerator froze. That lady never would go out with me again!

Soon after completing my degree and getting my first real job (post docs don't count), I again had the urge to drive a car. At the time, I had already been driving an electric car designed for people who are older. It had a top speed of 20 m.p.h. I wrote the local driving school (as my CP speech impedes telephone calls) and they dispatched a frightened young man in a car with no hand controls. Fortunately, he was able to refer me to a driving school that owned a car with hand controls. After many months of intermittent lessons, as I found every excuse to delay each lesson, I was finally ready to take the test. My teacher had prepared me well, but the Department of Motor Vehicles examiner was so nervous that he made me nervous. My driving teacher spent 10 minutes instructing the examiner in "Cerebral Palsy 101"; we were both relaxed and I passed the test with ease.

Buying a car wasn't easy. I took a friend with me; several people took him aside to try to convince him not to let me drive—as if anyone could stop me. I never thought I would meet a used car dealer who would try to avoid a sale. After I bought the car, I discovered that one insurance company even had special low rates for drivers with disabilities and good records.

Now came the hard part—telling my parents. Would you expect that a 30-year-old man with a Ph.D. and a full-time job as a social worker would be afraid to tell Mom and Dad that he was driving? I sure was! I piled my poor, chain-smoking, driving teacher into my "new" four-year-old American Motors Ambassador and drove the 50 miles to my parent's house. It's a good thing they both still had their original teeth, as anything else would have fallen out. They were both good sports about it, although, to this day, I prefer to have them drive if we go places together. Their nervousness about their son driving makes me nervous.

Driving did help me accomplish my original goal. It gave me mobility to make it easier to date. Five years later I met a wonderful lady. We are now married and she does the driving! The thrill of driving is gone; I guess that's a milestone too.

This article was first published in (date unknown) in Mainstream Magazine, *San Diego, CA. Reprinted with permission.*

Cerebral Palsy:
A Story of Deinstitutionalization
Age 33

I met Debbie while writing reports on the children in her living unit at an institution for people with developmental disabilities (about 1974). Generally, I do not have direct contact with the children, but in this case I was asked to become involved.

Debbie is a child who is 10-years-old, ambulatory, has cerebral palsy, and good self-help skills. She was diagnosed as severely cognitively impaired, but the treatment staff in the institution felt that her adequate development of self-help skills made the diagnosis questionable. Because she had no speech, and no other means of communication besides a few gestures, it was impossible to obtain a more accurate measure of Debbie's intelligence.

A staff member noted Debbie's extremely good eye contact, and saw it as a sign of higher intellectual functioning than previously diagnosed. On that basis, she was put into a sign language class where she rapidly developed the sign language ability of a child without cognitive delays. Later, several IQ tests showed that Debbie had normal intelligence, and her family requested that she return to their home.

Debbie was of particular interest to me because of our similar physical limitations. I was also once diagnosed with a cognitive disability. I met Debbie's parents at the time that the diagnosis of her "cognitive limitation" was being questioned. Debbie's living unit came under the sponsorship of a federal grant, which stipulated that the professional staff continue contact with children and their families after discharge.

Each time the family had a problem with Debbie, they called me. Since Debbie was discharged, the family has called me on the average of once a month, with one crisis after another. Some issues could be resolved by phone by giving them the information they needed. On other occasions I visited them in their home. The family's initial reaction to me was one of extreme gratitude, and the social distance between us soon disappeared as they discovered that people with cerebral palsy and Ph.D.s are just as human as everyone else.

Debbie was originally institutionalized because she had severe behavioral problems at home and at school. After she learned sign language, the behavior problems disappeared and have never reappeared again. We attribute this change to her ability to communicate her feelings in a socially acceptable manner.

When the family met me, they noted that Debbie's walking pattern was similar to mine, and that we had similar problems in manual dexterity. They were determined that if I could succeed in life, Debbie could also. We offered them the alternative of foster care placement, but they felt they could provide the motivation and support Debbie needed.

After the family learned sign language, they were better able to communicate with Debbie. Their ability to demonstrate affection for the child increased dramatically, but along with this came a feeling of helplessness, of what to do next.

Debbie's parents had a pretty clear concept of Debbie's original diagnosis, but they had not yet learned the wide variety of techniques for helping a child with CP and good cognitive functioning. They did not know how much Debbie could and could not do. They did not know what demands they could or could not make of her. They were concerned that she might become overtired and damage herself physically. They needed to learn to cope with Debbie's development, and they had great anxieties about her functioning in adolescence and adulthood.

When Debbie was originally diagnosed as cognitively limited, her mother felt she could get the best care in an institution, but without that diagnosis, they wanted her to be at home. But, they were now immobilized; their whole family life was disrupted. Their need was for information on how to cope with the "new" Debbie on a daily basis.

Debbie's mom was very concerned that Debbie might fall and injure herself irreparably. I explained how she had been taught to fall so that she would not. A person with cerebral palsy can learn to fall without getting hurt. Because of the extensive spasticity associated with cerebral palsy, many of us who walk have bones that are well-developed and do not break easily. The pressure of extremely spastic muscles against the bones assures development of a strong bone structure. Nonwalkers are much more likely to have weak bones.

Debbie's mother was also concerned that Debbie was overeating (particularly carbohydrates, especially bananas). I explained how carbohydrates meet the child's great energy needs, and that the bananas meet the typical cerebral palsy potassium shortage. I also suggested that the family look for high protein foods, which would help meet Debbie's health needs in the long run. I referred them to a pediatrician who cares for patients with cerebral palsy, and a dentist who treats such children.

We discussed what Debbie should and should not be allowed to do. There are many more "shoulds" than "should nots" relating to raising a child like Debbie. Some children are sheltered physically and psychologically much more than is wise. In terms of over-sheltering a child psychologically, parents are often afraid that able-bodied children and adults might say things which will upset their child.

It's my philosophy that if the child with CP receives the necessary love and support at home, he or she learns to cope with comments from the unenlightened public, both children and adults. Such a child can be taught to develop talents to compensate for a disability, and to make others aware of those compensating abilities.

In terms of physically overprotecting the child, this too can generally be handled by a social worker or other allied health professional. By spending time with the family in their home on an informal basis, it is not too difficult to observe instances of overprotection, and to make the parents and siblings aware of them.

For example, having watched Debbie pour her own milk at school, I was surprised to see her mother pouring it for her at home. I simply pointed out that Debbie could do it herself, and her mother needn't do it for her. Obviously, Debbie wasn't going to tell her mother about her ability as long as her mother waited on her.

Periodically, the family has crises related to Debbie. These are crises which any such family faces. They were very concerned about her lack of peer interaction while she attended a class for children who are deaf. She had been placed there because of her sign language skills, and her poor speech. These children all walked well, and could interact and play together more easily than Debbie could.

When she was able to develop enough speech to be placed in a class for children with cerebral palsy, where there were other children with similar ambulation problems, her peer interaction increased dramatically. Often crises have related to Debbie's ability to manipulate her parents in order to do things her way. My role has been to intervene and help reinforce the family's discipline, and to encourage them to make demands and to set limits.

Debbie's parents and I have discussed, on many occasions, the fact that there is no predicting what Debbie will be like as an adolescent or an adult. We know that the more work we do now, especially in the areas of speech and ambulation, the better off Debbie will be.

We set expectations for next month and for six months from now, but we know it's unwise to set expectations for adulthood that are specific to people with disabilities, except to provide her with information and about career opportunities in which she may be interested.

A most important part of my contact with this family has been my rapport with Debbie herself. The warm, personal relationship I have with Debbie has been a key to the development of my relationship with the family. Like any mother, Debbie's mom is more comfortable relating to someone who relates well with her child.

During the last year, I have changed the nature of our relationship by insisting on treating Debbie as the mature 10-year-old she is striving to be, rather than a cuddly five-year-old. At my suggestion, the family has followed suit.

At last contact, Debbie was reading and doing arithmetic just two years below expected grade level, which is a great accomplishment for a child who has only been out of such an institution for two years. Her family and peer relationships are improving.

A clinician would see my work with Debbie most clearly in terms of a role-modeling approach: that is, in terms of my being a role model for Debbie. I showed her how a handicapped person with a significant disability can and should relate to others.

Of equal significance, Debbie's parents saw me as a personal demonstration of what a person with a severe disability can accomplish. They began to see that what I had accomplished and what Debbie could also accomplish given the right opportunities. At the same time, they realized that it was important that they not attempt to make Debbie into a "carbon copy" of me.

On several occasions, I have helped the family in their negotiations with various people and organizations whose task it was to help Debbie. The family has had particular problems with public school teachers and administrators who did not make appropriate academic demands of Debbie. With my prodding, these people have realized Debbie's potential and have begun to relate to her in more appropriate ways.

Finally, I have worked with the family to help them learn to treat Debbie as a growing child rather than as a "phenomenon." Debbie may need some special attention because of her physical limitations, but most of all she needs to be treated as a human being with all the attributes and short-comings of any other human being.

We have not, and never will, solve all of Debbie's problems. People with physical disabilities and their families face challenges every day of their lives. My task, and that of other professionals who work with such people, is only to show them and their families how they can become as independent as possible, and to recognize, and deal appropriately with their own unique limitations and capabilities.

This article was first published in January of 1978 in Disabled USA, *Washington, DC. Reprinted with permission.*

Avoiding Administrative Stress and Executive Restrooms

Age 49 (Humor)

In the early 1990s, when the Department of Justice (DOJ) Administrator examination was announced, I started to complete the application. I needed time to decide if I really wanted to apply, so I put it aside and went off to a family reunion. I knew my family would have strong opinions; hopefully they would have some insights, too.

The first person I saw at the reunion hotel was my Uncle John, a retired actuary. Actuaries are statisticians who predict morbidity and mortality, an optimistic profession, if I say so myself. As soon as he started talking, I knew he was the wrong person to ask. He harangued me for an hour, quoting studies on job stress caused by IRS audits, used car salespeople, and administrative jobs. Has anyone ever studied the life expectancy of obnoxious actuaries? I'd begun to regret having mentioned the examination, when other relatives arrived and gave their reasons why this "aging hippie on wheels" might not make it as an administrator anywhere.

My cousin Jack, a retired manager from Ford who had supervised the construction of the Edsel, said that the necessary lifestyle changes would be too much of a shock. I would have to paint my ancient pickup truck so it wouldn't look like the property of an undercover agent. He also said that I'd have to shave my beard and buy a toupee. Jack couldn't tell me if I would have to pay less for a toupee, if I provided the hair from my beard.

My Aunt Patty put in her two cents worth. She said I'd be a poor administrator, remembering my childhood ineptitude at the game "telephone." Aunt Peggy said that when we played telephone as children, I could never remember to whisper. When it was my turn, everybody heard the secret and that spoiled the game.

My mother arrived then and told everyone that administrators have to keep secrets, and that's something I've never been good at. Thanks, Mom! It's not that I intentionally blab; it's that I forget what a secret is and what it isn't. Maybe I shouldn't have said that; now I'll never be offered a job at Scotland Yard, or in espionage.

My brother added that if I do become an administrator, I'd also have to learn to "fight constructively." He reminded me of a problem I had on my last job before I came to the California Department of Justice (DOJ). In that agency, my supervisor often chided me for being too agreeable, which meant I wasn't being "creative enough." Apparently, if you argue a lot you are "creative." They have you either way.

After that, my sister reminded me that administrators must wear ties most of the time. If I was promoted, my cleaning bill would soar (as I can only keep a tie clean for a few hours). No wonder my friend who owns a dry-cleaning shop keeps asking me when I will be promoted.

Finally, my cousin George, an executive in a manufacturing company in the East, arrived. He also uses a wheelchair and said that one of his problems in climbing the corporate ladder was that executive restrooms are super small. He got stuck in one in his wheelchair and had to wait for a group of super bigwigs to form a task force to determine the best way to dislodge him.

I thought about all this advice on the way home. Playing telephone never was much fun and my wheelchair has been trapped in enough gasoline station restrooms to last a lifetime. Maybe I'll pass on the DOJ Administrator I exam this time.

This article was first published in September of 1989 in DLE Update, *Sacramento, CA. Reprinted with permission.*

Getting Rich in the Lottery

Age 45

Peggy Pastel, my friend (the senior, and only, graphic artist who works in my department), is unlucky enough to have an office with a glass window, so everyone can see what she is doing. The other day I rolled by and saw her making faces and biting her tongue. She was annoyed at losing at lotto, and that made her hungry, which caused her to chew her tongue.

Peggy's chomping made me think that although playing the lottery should be encouraged because it helps our schools, losers should be compensated. People should feel good after they play, so they will want to play again. Then it came to me! Since losers are annoyed and hungry, why not give them something to eat? That is it—why not sell edible lottery tickets? If you lose, you just eat the ticket. Wouldn't you be more willing to buy a lottery ticket if you knew it would taste good? In fact, the state could contract with "31 Flavors" to make a ticket in every possible flavor.

Can't you just see all the people standing around the 7-Eleven eating their losing tickets after winning numbers have been announced? Someday that might be the "cool" place for singles to meet on Saturday night. Additionally, the monthly winner of our section's "Important Person Award" (who receives a lottery ticket) can describe the taste during the induction ceremony.

The State could make extra money by selling each ticket with an "A la mode option." That is, in case you lose, you automatically get a scoop of ice cream with each ticket. This option will also make your family happy, whether or not you win or lose, as long as you buy enough tickets a la mode for the whole family. Either you win the lottery or bring home edible tickets with ice cream. If my wife did that, I'd quit complaining about the low statistical probability of anyone ever winning the lottery.

Oh yes, just to please the liquor lobby, all the tickets will have a slightly salty flavor. That way when people go to 7-Eleven to buy lottery tickets, they will buy plenty of beer to go with them.

But best of all, this newly flavored lottery ticket will make me rich. I have submitted a suggestion form so that I will get a share of the state's profit from this idea. Now I can retire and write lurid fantasies. Look for my byline in future issues of *Playboy*.

Thank you, Peggy, for chewing your tongue and insuring my future prosperity.

This article was first published in January of 1988 in DLE Update, *Sacramento, CA. Reprinted with permission.*

How Many Ways Can You Get to Oakland by Wheelchair?

Ages 47 to 54

I often tell my readers about challenges that people with disabilities face in the 1990s. This time I describe several intercity public transportation problems for people with disabilities. If the discussion seems complex, bear with me as the problems themselves are indeed complex. Yet, I am proud of coping with these problems and successfully completing traveling assignments.

My work overseeing telephone services for California's Deaf and Disabled Telecommunications Program (DDTP) often takes me to Oakland. For several years, I have tried various transportation modes; I am searching for the fastest, cheapest, and easiest way to get there in an effort to save time and money for both the DDTP and me.

Flying is the fastest way to span most of the 80 miles between here and there, but the slowest way to cover the entire distance. That is because once I land at either end I must wait for ground transportation that is wheelchair accessible. There are no convenient flights into Oakland itself, so I fly to SF0 and catch a shuttle to BART; I exit BART three blocks from our Oakland office.

Flying makes me nervous, not because of the flight itself, but because most airlines are not equipped to ship my power wheelchair with its acid-filled batteries intact. Instead they must disassemble the chair, pack the batteries separately and reconnect them upon arrival. Not only does this take time, but includes the risk of being stranded at SF0 with a nonfunctioning wheelchair due to improper reassembly by the airlines. The one time I did fly, I spent eight hours of travel time for what would be a 90-minute car ride. This was not a good use of government time, but saving the government money has never been my ultimate goal.

It was really more fun to drive, as I had a driver who also went to graduate school in the 1960s, and trading war stories while she battled the traffic was fun. Those trips were also a great time to sleep. Sometimes I was the only person to arrive at the meetings wide awake. That gave me a great political advantage. Occasionally, I could get the committee to vote in favor of the speech disability budget, simply because my opposition kept falling asleep mid-sentence.

Traveling by Amtrak was also fun. I met very interesting people that way. It's too bad that I didn't have my nonprofit at that time as there were company executives who traveled between Sacramento and the Bay Area by Amtrak and I would have been able to hit them up for donations.

I never did travel by bus, because I understood that Greyhound always took apart power wheelchairs and I was afraid that they might not be able to get mine back together again. Besides that, I traveled with a terrier and I was afraid my terrier might not get along with Greyhounds. On the contrary, the Greyhound and the terrier might get along too well and the court might grant the Greyhound custody and make me responsible for "puppy support."

This article was first published (date unknown) in DLE Update, *Sacramento, CA. Reprinted with permission.*

If Today Is Sunday, I Must Be Home

Age 45

Much of my time at work now (1987) and at home is spent at a computer terminal writing or inputting data. You could probably determine my days off by examining my log on records in both computers. My job is a writing job, and at home I write a lot also. I am not a workaholic; I just enjoy writing and computers. At work, I write about crime statistics and disability issues for my employer. At home, I write letters and short articles, and play computer Scrabble. My computers and software at home and at work are similar, and the word processing software is identical. No wonder I don't know where I am half the time!

My interest in writing started in college. That was before computers, so since I cannot write legibly by hand because of cerebral palsy, I kept one electric typewriter in the boardinghouse, one in the library, and one in the dean's office for exams. Twelve hours a day of classes, studying, and writing papers was not unusual. There was little differentiation between work and play, since there was no time to play anyway.

Coming from a college environment into the working world was a shock for me. At first, I could not get used to working just eight hours a day—but somehow I managed! Now I must remind myself to be conscientious. Someday, my department may even have computerized thought auditors which will bleep every time my mind wanders—sort of a software version of Miss Hemlock, my fifth-grade teacher. "Bobbie keep your eyes on your paper, and your mind on your work." The poor lady never realized that I could pretend to do both.

I still cannot keep my work out of my home life, especially my dreams. The night we saw my supervisor in a restaurant, I dreamt that my wife and I were living in my office and every time we tried to kiss, my supervisor came in to ask for my weekly time sheet.

Of course, I occasionally have momentary office daydreams about home. The other day when the power went out for a few seconds and shut down my computer, some of my data were lost. I closed my eyes and counted to 10 to stem the frustration. I then pulled the office door open, as I would my study door at home. With my eyes still shut I called, "Did you run the toaster, disposal, and the VCR all at once again?"

When I opened my eyes, I turned six shades of red. My work was still on the screen with the changes of an hour ago, and my fingers were on the keyboard. Yet it was a different screen and keyboard. Instead of being at home, Monica (not Lewinski) of my department was standing at the copy machine, smiling quizzically.

What was going on? Had the power outage and the smell of the copy machine (which resembles burnt toast) combined to confuse me when I closed my eyes? Or was it just that I'd rather be home playing computer Scrabble, than be at work writing a report and smelling the copy machine?

So friends, be careful and figure out where you are before you speak. Keep your work life at work and your home life at home. And don't yell at Monica unless you are her husband—and she really does turn on the toaster, the VCR, and the disposal all at once!

This article was first published in November of 1987 in DLE Update, *Sacramento, CA. Reprinted with permission.*

My Great Business Venture

Age 34

At lunch in the cafeteria, people often discuss their business ventures. I was eating lunch with my friends, Stan, Mark, and Charlie. Stan does well with real estate; Mark has been successful writing software; and Charlie has landed squarely on his feet in a number of business projects.

Back in 1976, I, too, tried my hand at business, but with questionable results. It was Ben, an enterprising engineering student, who got me started. He seemed to know quite a bit about making money, and he became my teacher. I first hired Ben to help me around the house a few hours a day, but he soon discovered that he needed more work than that. Our solution was for me to buy a rooming house and have Ben manage it so he could make a living of sorts. Since I needed a live-in helper anyway, a few additional people in the house would not disrupt my privacy. Or so I thought. Ben and I chose a house only a mile from my office, as I am a persistent dawdler, and this was one way to be sure that I got to work on time. It was also only three miles from the local junior college, to assure the availability of tenants.

The house was a standard, three-bedroom tract home at the end of a cul-de-sac called Greenhorn Drive (a name which probably made all four of my immigrant grandparents chortle in their graves). We chose that location so that the tenants' cars would not irritate the neighbors. This was a good idea because our tenants (mostly college students) often repaired their cars in front of our house, leaving them there in various states of disassembly for months at a time.

College students made ideal tenants because their lack of money obliged them to tolerate the limited accommodations which we provided. Such accommodations were indeed limited only by our entrepreneurial zeal. Ben and I hired a nonunion carpenter to use 2 x 4s and drywall to subdivide our living room and den into three of the tiniest bedrooms you have ever seen. That gave me a total of four bedrooms to rent out at $60 a piece, which more than covered my $227.00 house payment.

The place was always cluttered and filthy, given the housekeeping habits of college students. Every time I hired cleaning people, Ben found a reason to dismiss them. I was his best friend and he didn't want me wasting my money. People from the county health department sometimes left reminders to dispose of garbage, which accumulated in paper bags in the garage. My tenants and I could never agree on whose turn it was to take the garbage out to the curb. Nor could any of us remember which night to put it out, despite the presence of all our neighbors' garbage cans on the curb on the appropriate night.

Fortunately, this great entrepreneurial enterprise ended before either the health department or the zoning authority called us to task. I had excellent motivation for going out of business. I had just become engaged, and that was reason enough to kick out the roomers, remove the partitions, and turn the house into a clean and comfortable place for the two of us to live.

I don't think I was meant to be a business person. Owning a rooming house just isn't the easiest road to riches anyway.

This article was first published in February of 1990 in DLE Update, *Sacramento, CA. Reprinted with permission.*

Stop Kicking the Copy Machine

Age 46

My office opens onto the office copy machine, and just watching everyone in my department use it is like sitting in Times Square and watching everyone you have ever known walk by. This complicated and often unreliable machine is a great equalizer, frustrating office assistants and bureau chiefs with equal ease. In effect, it harasses everyone but no one can file a grievance. One of my current favorite pastimes (1988) is to open my door at lunch and watch the machine abuse people.

Its victims have a variety of emotional reactions. Many people even have a love-hate relationship with the machine, addressing it with obscenities or sweet cooing sounds, depending upon its behavior. Some users are bossy, others are angry, and many are just curious. Practical users read the instructions before attempting to use the machine, but other approaches vary. I watched one man fill a whole wastebasket with bad copies in his determination to make the machine work right without reading instructions. Occasionally, people kick the machine or psychoanalyze it. Some athletic employees jump up and down in front of it, while religious ones appear to pray to it.

Many people are impressed with our copier's unusual abilities. I was thrilled to learn that it would copy both sides of a piece of paper. I kept waiting for it to toss pages in the air in order to copy the other side, like a cook tossing flapjacks. In addition, it can copy the "whole thing" in one operation and never need Rolaids the next day.

There's only one real problem with our copier; it is designed for people to use while standing. I can't reach it easily from my wheelchair. To use a copier, one choice is to go all the way to the end of the block-long corridor and stop at the cafeteria for a cold drink and a chat. What a chore! Of course, the state could buy a power wheelchair with a vertical lift for using tall copiers. My other choice is to schmooze someone else into doing my copying because I can't reach the buttons. I am often asked if I mind the noisy office copier, but I like having my office in the back of the unit far away from departmental politics. Besides that, the copier's entertainment value far outweighs its liabilities. The noise of the copier keeps me awake when my work is dull, and if my work gets difficult.

This article was first published in October of 1988 in DLE Update, Sacramento, CA. Reprinted with permission.

The Year 2022: Looking Back at Technology in Our Future

Age 46

In retrospect, 2022 was a great year (or so I speculated when I wrote this piece about 1988). I turned 80 and celebrated my 50th year of state employment. It's amazing how much things have changed here in the last half century, especially for employees with disabilities.

While I still drive my own van with hand controls to work sometimes, if I am lazy, I program it to go from home to work without consulting me. On still other days, I fly to work.

Some of us who began Transcendental Meditation when the Beatles did back in the 1960s have perfected Maharishi's flying technique to get to work using "Mantra Power" alone!

Last year, reincarnation enabled Harold Sparks (one of the department's first wheelchair-using employees) to rise from the dead and reinstate. "Old Sparky" ran successfully for governor and balanced the budget with a super tax on fast food. In 1999, disabled employees reached parity and the Limited Examination and Appointment Program (LEAP) was abolished. LEAP was a program for facilitating access to state employment for people with disabilities.

That year a new Reasonable Accommodation standard was set when Joe Montana got a new robot-like body to attach to his old head and became the first 90% synthetic quarterback. That same year, Andrew Absolute, a holier-than-thou co-worker, transferred back here from the Department of Drug and Alcohol Abuse to institute our division's Coffee Abstinence Program (CAP), forbidding employee abuse of caffeine.

Our building's new security system automatically reads employee fingerprints and opens the outside doors for us. We wheelchair users were especially glad to have this system. That is because the system only works with automatic doors so the Division finally had to install doors that open automatically, just like the kind that supermarkets got 40 years ago. While the Disabled Employees Advisory Committee has requested them every year since 1985, somehow the funding has never materialized until now, despite the ADA.

In 1998, the time interchange system replaced the standard 40-hour work week. This system uses a headband which automatically reads our brain waves and tells us when we have finished thinking about work-related matter after putting in the required 40 hours.

Another new technology is the personal temperature control unit. This solar-powered unit sets up a temperature ring, or aura, around your body; everything within that ring can be set at a desired temperature. This is much cheaper than heating and cooling every office suite.

But my personal favorite new technology is the computerized speech interpreter. This wallet-sized gem listens to my cerebral-palsied speech and repeats everything I say in clear, precise English. One disadvantage of my new voice is that people always understand me right off. I can no longer change my mind and take my foot out of my mouth when someone does not understand a rash comment on my first try.

All in all, 2022 has been a great year. Next year will be even better. With Cher as our country's new president and Ralph Nader as vice-president, we have four good years to look forward to.

This article was first published (date unknown) in DLE Update, *Sacramento, CA. Reprinted with permission.*

Writing "Just" for Fun?

Age 47

During lunch hour today (I wrote in 1989), I helped Susan Studious, a clerk in the next office edit a theme for her American history class at City College. She hates to write and asked why I volunteer to write for the *DLE Update*. I said that my column for the *Update* requires a kind of writing that is both fun and an "ego trip." It reminds me of third grade, when my favorite time was "Show and Tell."

Writing these columns is also fun because it makes people laugh. No one, besides me, says that my column must be funny, yet I could no more write a humorless column than I could fly. As you would expect, I write my best humor without trying, and when I try to be funny, my mind goes blank. Remember being on a first date and trying to think of funny things to say just to ease the tension? It's the same problem; I must wait for ideas to come to me. Complying with a self-imposed "funny rule" every month could be my undoing.

With another 15 years to retirement, I would like to write 180 more funny columns without seriously offending anyone. If that prospect doesn't scare me into some serious joke writing, nothing will. Can anybody suggest ideas for columns? I'll give you a free wheelchair ride! Also, remember that all employees are encouraged to write articles for the *DLE Update*. Your pieces are most welcome. The more people who contribute, the better a newsletter we will have.

Unfortunately, the most likely place for my ideas to pop up is in the shower. The problem is how to write these ideas down before they slip down the drainpipe with the water. If you've ever seen me writing at a desk, just imagine my problems writing in the shower. Oh well, someday computers will be waterproof, and I can "word-process" under water to my heart's content. Gurgle! Gurgle!

After finishing a column, I ask several people to read it. A loving, but firm, censor and humor critic (my best friend) usually keeps me out of trouble. I try not to make fun of anybody, except myself and my friends, but sometimes it's tempting. Anything she misses, our staff editor generally catches. You may wonder why I use so many readers, but once I was attacked by an English teacher who came charging at me carrying six double negatives and a poison split infinitive. The assault kept me away from my keyboard for a month and caused me to pepper everything I wrote with commas for another six weeks. You can never be too careful with your punctuation!

These kind readers also occasionally catch inappropriate sexy and sexist remarks that slip by me. Yet such remarks are just my way of correcting the generally asexual media image of people with disabilities. Even Ironsides never had a steady woman friend! Somebody has to start breaking down these stereotypes.

Don't you think that my humor column is a great place to initiate a change in world thinking about sex and people with disabilities?

So you see, I told Susan Studious, writing my column for the *DLE Update* is fun, an ego trip—and even a little sexy sometimes. Now back to your description of Aaron Burr's thesis on the evils of dueling. In the second sentence of the third paragraph I think I spot a dangling modifier.

This article was first published in August of 1990 in DLE Update, *Sacramento, CA. Reprinted with permission.*

A Real Picnic

Age 49

Peggy Pastel, our graphic artist, was looking quizzical as I rolled by her office. She called me in, because the Director's Office had asked her to help think up a new theme for the annual (about 1991) department picnic. After all, the picnic is coming soon.

Apparently, just because I can write silly stories, she thought I might be good at this too. Well, I really could not help her, but I did manage to think up themes for some picnics that might have been planned by U.S. Presidents and other famous people.

For example, FDR's picnic would have had to have been planned a year in advance by the Works Picnic Administration, but Truman's picnic would have been planned on the spur of the moment during a morning walk. Nixon might have bugged the ants at his picnic and Karl Marx would have never permitted a picnic as they are "the opiate of the ants." The staunch anti-communist of the 1950s, Senator Joseph McCarthy, would have banned ketchup from his picnic because it is red.

While President Carter would have served his guests peanuts and Billy Beer, President Grant would have served something stronger. Ollie North would plan a picnic strictly according to regulation, but only for him and his secretary, Fawn Hall.

Such picnics would have varied enormously in cost; thus, British Prime Minister Chamberlain would have had "A Picnic at Any Cost," and Herbert Hoover's picnic would have been paid for by free enterprise. Jack Kennedy, on the other hand, would have shamed his guests into bringing everything themselves by telling them to "Ask not, what your picnic can do for you."

Some picnics would have had specific themes. Of course, the 1950s presidential candidate Adlai Stevenson, would have asked everyone to come to "A Picnic in Stocking Feet." That is because he often forgot to have his shoes repaired. Once he even crossed his legs on TV showing his socks through a hole in his shoe. Teddy Roosevelt would have advised his guests to cook their hot dogs softly, but carry a big fly swatter. Everyone would be asked to bring shovels to George Washington's picnic in order to help plant cherry trees, and they would have to bring shovels to LBJ's picnic for another reason. Mrs. Reagan might plan a "picnic in the stars." Of course, I would recommend a Scrabble picnic.

Well, now that we know how all those famous people would have run their picnics, can anyone suggest a theme for our departmental one? If so, please tell Peggy Pastel—before she starts smoking again from trying to think of a theme—or we'll just have to call it "Dr. Bob's Picnic."

This article was first published (date unknown) in DLE Update, *Sacramento, CA. Reprinted with permission.*

Chapter Five

Humor

My sense of humor has been my great ally;
Mom says that I began telling puns at age 4.
For many years, I created and wrote the humor
column in the California Division of Law
Enforcement (DLE) Newsletter. Some of those
columns that were particularly funny are included
in this section. One of my contributions to DLE
was to teach my fellow employees about my joy of
life despite my disability.

On the Streets of Sacramento

Age 47

When we moved to Sacramento, I thought that this would be an easy city to navigate. All the streets are named A, B, C in one direction and 1st, 2nd, 3rd in the other. Little did I know that Sacramento has many confusing one-way streets, and for no reason many streets change names unexpectedly. P Street becomes Stockton Boulevard, Capitol Avenue becomes Folsom, and J Street becomes Fair Oaks Boulevard. I was used to the problem of one-way streets, as I had lived in Waterbury, Connecticut, where the extremely narrow downtown streets were laid out before the coming of the automobile. However, this business of streets that change names unexpectedly makes no sense.

When a friend described a similar, but much more complex problem in London, England, I mentioned my consternation with Sacramento Street names. My friend let me know that I was exaggerating the problem in Sacramento. He said, "London is to Sacramento, as Kafka is to Walt Disney." His meaning was clear, after I dug out my college literary textbook from 25 years ago, which described Kafka as a bizarre, turn of the century, German fiction author who wrote complex, often incomprehensible, prose based on his tortured mental state. (That also sounds like an apt description of the state of my mind and the quality of my writing during my college years.)

Even if Sacramento streets are not as confusing to navigate as London's, many of them do have funny and misleading names. Elsewhere in the city, the names of other Sacramento streets raise questions. How many hazelnuts live on Hazel Nut Lane? How many villas are there on Villa Drive, or did realtors just name it that to lure prospective buyers into fantasizing about building villas there? Do the atomic particles inside automobile tires cause many blow outs on Los Alamos Drive? How rustic is Carmichael's Rustic Road?

Closer to our office, Fairgrounds Drive is where the fairgrounds were, not where they are now. I like to say that the elevator I take is where the ferris wheel was. That way I can say that where people used to go "up, up, and away," they now get off at the second floor. I also like to tell people that the street address of our building was chosen not by the post office or the city, but by a group of 49er fans who said that the redundancy (4949) was needed for emphasis.

The one street name I have never come across in Sacramento or in my trips around the country is Bob Segalman Street. Now that is one street name that makes sense. Let me know if you spot it anywhere. I'd settle for just Segalman Street!

This article was first published in April of 1989 in DLE Update, *Sacramento, CA. Reprinted with permission.*

Oxymoron Heaven

Age 48

I was "clearly confused" when the car salesman said that my new van required a "low raised" roof, to accommodate my "moderately tall" wheelchair. But when he mumbled something about an "oxymoron," I wondered why he was calling a paying customer a stupid ox. Reaching for my unabridged Webster's dictionary from the "maxi glove compartment" of my wheelchair, I read that an oxymoron is a "figure of speech" that combines contradictory ideas.

Our vocabulary is full of oxymorons which even invade the language of our "political leadership's" "political promises." "Benevolent politicians" often create self-contradictory expressions like "social security" and "federal assistance," but now we have a name for them. President George H. W. Bush promised us a quieter, gentler time. Since the Republicans couldn't keep that promise, they used "precise oxymorons" to give us a quieter, gentler vocabulary. Of this, "concerned citizens" can be "fairly certain."

We now live in a "free society," which is becoming known for its "public relations" and its "undisguised double speak." Of course, most societies claim to be free, even those with "benevolent dictators." One friend, who teaches college English, said that even the word "free" is an oxymoron. She provided a "brief analysis" of this "applied theory," while we waited at the IRS to pay additional taxes through "voluntary compliance" to avoid "involuntary incarceration." Of course, we could have avoided this problem if we had used the "artificial intelligence" in our "personal computers" to more "accurately estimate" our "voluntary obligations."

How strange that Miss "Joy Hemlock," my fifth-grade English teacher, excluded oxymorons from her "lecture discussions." But then maybe I was "busy listening" to my "inner voice." Or as my pal, "Will Knot," said when Miss Hemlock asked him where his grammar was, "Oh, she's home knitting." But he often gave "ambiguous answers" to her frequent "unanswerable questions," posed after lining us up "alphabetically according to height" in "reverse order."

Oxymorons provide gentle ways of conveying harsh reality. Doctors describe impending death as "limited life expectancy" and automobile salespeople describe tin cans as "compact cars" or "mini-vehicles." They also describe El Caminos and Rancheros as "gentlemen's pickups," which I always thought were high-priced prostitutes. Even we criminal statisticians have oxymorons, like "involuntary manslaughter," "petty theft," "simple assault," and "statutory rape."

My "ambiguous knowledge" of oxymorons prompted the following attempt to break the world's record for the most oxymorons used in one paragraph: Joe's "family vacation" by "light rail" on the "Little Big Horn" resulted in an "amicable divorce" after "military intelligence" described his "slightly pregnant" wife as an "unfaithful lover." They found her "panty hose" in the "brief case" of an "intimate stranger" after an evening of "sweet torture." Joe sat eating "fresh frozen" "jumbo shrimp" and "meatless meat" in "thunderous silence" drowning his "sweet sorrow" in "light beer" and "reaffirming his faith" in "serial monogamy." This was not a "new experience" for him as he often ate "gourmet diet food" in his "mobile home" at his "genuine lucite" table with "plastic silverware."

I'll conclude with my brother Dan's "almost perfect" definition of an oxymoron, obtained at the University of Texas (UT), Austin. UT's rivals are the Texas Aggies whose intelligence the UT students often "gently disparage." With "puny humor" Dan defined an oxymoron as: an Aggie in an acid bath. Of course, he told this story while riding in a "mini-bus" powered by "dry ice" to preserve "clean air." (When Dan read this paragraph, he asked me if I invented the concept of a dry ice powered vehicle. Of course, I did.)

This article was first published in April of 1990 in DLE Update, *Sacramento, CA. Reprinted with permission.*

Scrabble Addiction

Ages 13 to 46

My love affair with Scrabble began one hot August day late in Eisenhower's first term, when my Uncle Max brought a set home to take his mind off of national politics. Uncle Max was a frustrated Stevenson Democrat who complained that, because Ike was giving the American people everything they wanted, the Democrats would never regain control of Congress. He drowned his frustration in Scrabble and beer, and got me hooked on Scrabble as I was too young for beer.

Most of my friends know of my fascination with Scrabble, so when our section's computer whiz found a Scrabble game that I could play on my home computer, he told me right away. That very day I picked up the Scrabble disk at Egghead Software, which one friend says is a perfect place for a Ph.D. to shop.

Most of my life I've had trouble finding Scrabble partners when Uncle Max wasn't around. My dad stopped playing with me after he lost three or four times. Mom plays occasionally but without enthusiasm. How much pride can you take in your son's victories when you're always the loser? I remember whole weekends in the early 1970s spent driving from one end of Los Angeles County to the other just for a Scrabble game.

The night I bought the game, I gobbled my dinner so I could begin playing. The game has eight skill levels, each with a larger dictionary and more advanced playing strategy. After two weeks of nightly games, I can just beat the computer at level 7, and I am reluctant to go on to level 8. Why should I go to bed a loser, when at level 7 I can always doze off a winner? A few more weeks of winning though, and I should be ready for the new challenge.

My success at level 7 means that the manufacturer has obviously rigged the game to flatter the average player's ego given my modest performance in local club tournaments. My success at computer Scrabble may also reflect the fact that I cheat. As I play, I thumb through my official Scrabble dictionary and list of 85 acceptable two-letter words from "aa" (a Hawaiian word for solidified lava) to "ye" (an archaic form of l). Since the computer has a complete dictionary in its memory, it's only fair for me to use one. I never play against the clock. That would be unfair since the computer can think so fast.

Computer Scrabble has numerous advantages over the traditional kind. The computer rarely takes a long time to make a word, and never bites its nails or makes clicking sounds with its teeth when I take a long time. And when it is losing, it never blows smoke in my face as one of my human competitors is prone to do. Beware however, that computer Scrabble is addictive. Now I have a better idea of what our Narcotic Control Section is up against. I've even thought about playing on my computer at work during lunch, however, once before my boss threatened to audit my hard disk and report any misuse of state property to management.

Well. You'll have to excuse me. My supper is digested now, and I hear my Scrabble disk calling. Oh yes, don't play computer Scrabble too soon after eating, you'll get brain cramps.

This article was first published in February of 1988 in DLE Update, *Sacramento, CA. Reprinted with permission.*

Vanity Plates

Missive: I wrote this piece in 1989 at age 47.

During my lunch hour, I get sunshine in our parking lot. I often smile at people's creativity in choosing vanity license plates. I've seen plates like: CEMEGO, BLUVYU, LUVS1K, and PAIDFOR. Other plates my friends have spotted include: FURCOAT, BADBOY, IAMB4U and T42AT3. My all time favorite plate was on an old VW that read 4US2CRUZ.

License plates often advertise the driver's occupation. One graduate social worker had the plate MSW78. Similarly, an optometrist had the plate I DOC. Somebody has the plate RABBI, and my brother Dan saw a New Mexico plate that read VIOLIST. There is nothing like having your resume on your license plate. Perhaps these people expect job offers during freeway gridlocks. Other plates advertise businesses; one real estate broker's plate read BUYAHOME. On the contrary, some people choose license plates to compensate for their professions such as the dentist with the plate FRIEND. Maybe he wanted people to know that he wasn't such a bad guy even if he drilled teeth all day.

A funny license plate suggestion came from my 12-year-old niece, Becky, whose family owns three ancient Volvos: a red one that she called CATSUP, a yellow one called MUSTARD, and a gray one with numerous red rust spots called RELISH. San Francisco *Chronicle* writer Herb Caen cited the most daring plate I've heard of: GR8NBED on a "Pontiac Fiero driven by a beauty." I hope no DMV staff got in trouble for letting that one get by. Caen also saw ME N MY on a Dodge Shadow.

Caen wrote that an El Cerrito firm called POETIC LICENSE will choose a clever plate for you for $15, or $30 for the cleverness plus the DMV paperwork to obtain the plate. That firm chose 2 AT1CE for a family of twins.

As I am currently buying a van, it seemed a good time to express my vanity and choose an individualized license plate too. The list of possibilities was amusing. During the elimination process, I vetoed one friend's suggestion that my plate should read PHERD, since a PHERD is a nerd with a Ph.D.

Speaking of Ph.D.s, as of July 1988, the DMV listed over 100 license plates beginning with PHD in its three-volume book, "Environmental License Plate Numbers." California sure has plenty of vain scholars. I saw the DMV's second volume listing license plates IMPVSR through RKSONE including IMSHURE, LIBERAL, LIC2LUV, LIBRA, and IMRRGHT. If that last driver is "right," why did he or she spell "right" "rrght?"

I almost chose license plates with only my initials on them, but my driver refused to cruise around town in a van with the insignia BS on its front and rear bumper. She thought the plate should read GOFERSHOFER. Yet that was longer than the DMV allows and GO4SHO4 was too difficult to decipher. I also excluded plates with job references as they might confuse the public. For example, I vetoed SAC-ER as one who works for the Statistical Analysis Center, not one who bags groceries. I considered plates symbolizing my hometown, PEORIAN. You'll know my final decision when you see my new van arrive at work someday soon, assuming I complete the DMV paperwork to order the plates.

This article was first published (date unknown) in DLE Update, *Sacramento, CA. Reprinted with permission.*

A Funny Thing Happened
in the Shower

Age 63
A Note to Management:

I always like to write memos to "management," as nobody really knows who management is and that way no one gets offended. On that note,

I woke up early this morning and was looking forward to my shower. It occurred to me that I think best in the shower, so I took an extra long shower to see what would come to mind. I couldn't do that when I was married, as my ex always banged on the door to see if I was OK.

The idea that came to me this morning was that perhaps moist heat increases one's thinking power. So does that mean that by the year 3,000, we will all have moisture-producing electrodes implanted in our brains and we all will think like Einstein? If so, the only thing that people would ever talk about would be the Theory of Relativity. How boring.

Suddenly, as I dried myself, the doorbell rang, and then it rang again. Hmm, could it be the mail carrier? I remember the Broadway play *The Postman Always Rings Twice*. Then out of nowhere, two attractive women appeared at my bathroom door. I grabbed a towel to pretend that I was modest. This is every man's dream. Two women at once and I was stark naked! This is a great place to live, but do they really offer such services?

Right away, they brought me my voice output device. Apparently, I had stayed in the shower too long, as there was water leaking into the apartment below me. Hurrah! Again, we have verified the law of gravity.

(I am surprised that law got passed, given the recent log jam in Congress.)

I guess I will have to take short showers and go out in the rain without a hat to test my theory. Perhaps that justifies a trip to Hawaii, where the rain is warm.

Unpublished, written in 2007.

Chapter Six
Disability Activism

I have advocated for the rights of people with disabilities all my life. My efforts are described in this section. I managed to incorporate my activism into several of my jobs, much to the distress of management. My own career would have been much less stressful without my activism, but it would also have been less rewarding. Even though during much of that time disability rights were not yet established, I benefited from the already established rights of women and minorities. Management and others generally gave me the benefit of the doubt when I made requests based on those rights extended to people with disabilities.

Never Ride a Paratransit to an APTA Demonstration

Age 45

Recently, I traveled to a rally of people with disabilities at the San Francisco meeting of the American Public Transit Association (APTA). The trip taught me a great deal about the necessity for wheelchair accessible fixed-route transportation such as trains and city buses with wheelchair lifts.

I never planned to attend the demonstration, because the 100-mile drive has become more difficult with advancing arthritis. I changed my mind when the editor of a national disability magazine hinted she might publish an article if I wrote about it. (As a Ph.D., I seek opportunities to publish with great tenacity.)

When a local agency offered its "paratransit" type mini-van and driver to persons wanting to attend the demonstration, I thought my problems were solved. Actually this was an unusual offer in that Paratransit is limited to fixed routes; but the company owner supported our cause. Their offer also sounded strange after my 1960s days of student activism, because in those days, that company would have been considered a part of "the establishment" and would never have made such an offer.

Paratransit is a system of mini-vans that provides door-to-door transportation by appointment for people with disabilities. I'd never ridden paratransit, so I still had to learn its problems:

- A primary problem with daily paratransit use is the time lost and lack of rider control over his or her own time, making it almost impossible for someone to use paratransit on a daily basis for business purposes.

- With bathroom stops and time spent picking up other passengers at their houses, the usual two-hour trip from Sacramento to San Francisco took an additional hour.

- Priorities other than original schedule or rider's need often take precedence.

- Conflicts arise between riders over use of travel time. Travel time allows me to catch up on reading, paperwork, or lost sleep, while for many Paratransit riders, travel time provides one of their few opportunities to socialize. A city bus or train might be as noisy, but hopefully lonely passengers would be more restrained about initiating undesired socialization. Given the wide variety of educations, interests, and lifestyles of people riding paratransit vehicles, why should they be denied the anonymity which riders of other public transit enjoy?

- The paternalistic relationship between driver and rider is demeaning. This relationship fosters dependence when the rider seeks independence. Although public transit insurance regulations stipulate that the driver must load my wheelchair and check my seat belt, in the informality of paratransit I fear that he might also try to brush my teeth.

- The need to reserve a ride in advance puts a burden on the paratransit rider which no other local public transit user faces. No one can reasonably run their lives with that kind of advanced planning.

Conclusion

We know the time, expense, and political change required to establish fixed route accessible transportation. These are not something we can expect soon. Yet they are something for which we must continue to strive.

This article was first published in November of 1987 in Mainstream Magazine, *San Diego, CA; then republished in October of 1989 in* DLE Update, *Sacramento, CA. Reprinted with permission.*

A Funny Thing Should Have Happened at Friends State College

Missive: This chapter is both fictional and full of very dry humor. You may want to read it while sitting next to a humidifier.

During the summer of 1969, before Spiro Agnew discovered nolo contendre and Richard Nixon discovered the tape-recorder, Friends State College established a Disabled Students Committee (DSC). I chaired the committee at this small Midwestern college. After its first year of operation, the college asked me to report its progress to an oversight committee of faculty and deans.

The meeting with the committee started out well, but some people fidgeted. I settled into a high-backed chair, brought in especially for my sore neck, and listened to various reports. This was a particularly somber group and their mood became more apparent when I distributed my two-page DSC Report for them to read. The report first discussed the college's recent survey to enumerate students with disabilities. I then jokingly suggested more effective ways to increase the number of registered students with disabilities:

1. We could register everyone who limped on the way to class on Monday morning as either arthritic or hung over.

2. We could visit all the classrooms and announce, in a quiet voice, that all students would receive a tuition reduction (from the money which the county received from selling confiscated homemade whiskey, back to the out of state farmers who made it in the first place). Anyone who didn't laugh would be registered as hearing impaired. Any student who didn't smile when we issued tuition reduction notices the following week would be classified as sight impaired or depressed.

I looked around the conference table watching people's eyes move down the page, past that paragraph. To my amazement, no one laughed! They just kept fidgeting. They went on reading about DSC's goal to teach all students more about those of us with disabilities. Such programs would include discussion of various disabilities, plus an exercise in which participants would ride in a wheelchair for an hour or be led around the block blindfolded. In the report, I suggested that the simulations should more realistically approximate working conditions for students with disabilities. For example:

- To experience a speech disability, I would tell a student to put two Ping-Pong balls in his or her mouth and then pretend to try to explain to a professor (who had a migraine) why a term paper was late.

- To experience a hearing loss, I would ask a student to put cotton in his or her ears and simulate an oral examination. The examiners would be instructed to intermittently look away or cover their mouths while speaking.

- To experience using a wheelchair, I would ask a student to sit in a power wheelchair and simulate a meeting with a visiting dignitary to the college. The wheelchair's motor would be rigged to die, while the dignitary watched the employee try to leave the room as the meeting ended.

Still no one laughed. They finished reading my report without a smile and continued to fidget uncomfortably. As we prepared for lunch, I gathered my papers together, rested for a minute in the comfortable high-backed chair and watched as the committee stood to leave. They were such a somber group.

Why are able-bodied people often embarrassed when people with disabilities tell jokes about disability in their presence? Why must such jokes be told when no one with a disability is around? How come, only then, will able-bodied people allow themselves to laugh? When able-bodied people can laugh with me about some aspect of my disability, it usually means that we are friends.

This article was first published (date unknown) in DLE Update, *Sacramento, CA. Reprinted with permission.*

Movie Review of "My Left Foot"

Age 47

Perhaps once in a lifetime, one goes to the movies and finds oneself looking in the mirror. For me, "My Left Foot" provides that experience. This movie is the biography of a fellow member of that very small group of people with severe cerebral palsy (CP) who have successfully led mainstream professional and personal lives. This movie is all about Christy Brown who was unable to walk, speak clearly, or control his arm and finger movements because of CP. Unlike half the CP population, Brown was not cognitively impaired; although his severe physical limitations made him appear so to the inexperienced eye (as do mine).

The movie "My Left Foot" portrays condescending treatment which many of us still receive from members of the medical and allied professions, the public, and often family and friends. In such situations, I flaunt my Ph.D., but Christy Brown had no such recourse. The movie included many references to Brown's strong romantic and sexual interest. I wonder why men with CP often develop a reputation for having strong sexual drives? Perhaps many men with disabilities seek that reputation to combat the societal stereotype that people with disabilities are asexual. After all, even television's most famous wheelchair user, Ironsides, never had a regular woman companion.

This cultural stereotype is reflected in the movie's inclusion of only one truly romantic scene, which is a major fault of the presentation. The movie gave extensive treatment to Brown's sexuality in the abstract, but showed almost no necking. It did show Brown's many flirtations, but nothing more graphic than a kiss. After the film ended, a statement flashed on the screen giving the date of Brown's wedding. Scenes from the wedding itself and a brief view of the honeymooners kissing in bed would have been most welcome. Christy, and the rest of us with CP, would probably not stay married long, if our spouses were only willing to recognize our sexuality in the abstract as this film does.

As for Brown's alcohol abuse, alcoholism was a part of his life and culture independent of his cerebral palsy. The film shows Brown in several alcoholic rages, one in a bar where he kicks a man in the groin after the offender belittles Brown for his disability. I hope that viewers will not associate severe CP with alcoholism, although alcoholism is not unknown within the population.

Brown had a more extensive physical disability than most of the CP population. He and I are among a small percentage of people with CP with total body involvement.

Brown was born in 1932 to a poor, alcoholic, Irish bricklayer. He received no formal education, physical therapy, or any of the other training now available to children with CP. The movie appears to accurately portray growing up with severe CP in Ireland in the 1930s and 1940s where such resources were scant. Brown educated himself with some outside encouragement once he discovered how to write, type, and paint with the toes of his left foot. He resorted to this technique as his flailing, uncontrollable arms and hands were almost useless. Brown wrote and illustrated a book about his early life called "My Left Foot." He also wrote several novels.

The film shows Brown's mistreatment by people who saw him as cognitively impaired because of his flailing movements and speech limitations. Such people often talked about him disparagingly in front of him as if he were deaf, an insult which I often encounter. Brown died in 1981 at age 48 by choking on his food; I've slowed my eating pace since learning that. Had Brown lived, he would have been a member of the first generation of people with severe CP not likely to die at a young age from respiratory ailments. The invention of antibiotic medication will allow our generation to live to old age in large numbers. On the contrary, Brown's early death may have spared him from suffering from the mistakes which the medical profession will inevitably make in their attempts to care for such unusual patients in middle and old age.

Unfortunately, Brown's early death prevented him from benefiting from the computer age, which has done so much to help people with severe CP. For example, he wrote without a word processor, and using a typewriter must have reduced his output considerably as it did mine. He probably could have written much more if he were alive today. Had he lived to the year 2020, he might have had access to a computer which could understand his garbled speech and output a clear version. In conclusion, film goers should note that Brown was not one of a kind. Besides myself, I know many other people in this country who will watch "My Left Foot" and feel as if they are looking in the mirror. That is, there are other people with severe CP who have married and established careers in the professions. Several other people with CP have also published autobiographies. Unfortunately, their literary agents and publishers were not as successful as Brown's was.

This article was first published in May of 1989 in DLE Update, *Sacramento, CA. Reprinted with permission.*

Chapter Seven
Medical

More is known today about cerebral palsy than when I was a child. These chapters describe my experiences receiving medical care as a child and an adult. Having an iconoclast like me as a patient was not always fun for the doctors and therapists who cared for me. At age 6, for example, I was surprised how furious I made my physical therapist. She left me on the mat on the floor to exercise while she answered the telephone 5 feet away. Not wanting to be ignored, I crawled over and looked up her skirt.

Contradictions in Mental Health Care

(Or, No Reason Not to Seek Help)

Age 49

Over the last three years, I have benefited enormously from personal counseling (also called psychotherapy). Such counseling is available to all state employees and paid for in part through the Employee Assistance Program (EAP) and the mental health services included in our medical insurance. My positive experience prompts me to remind you of both the availability of this resource and some of its potential drawbacks and contradictions. I am describing these drawbacks not to discourage you from seeking help, but to give you more insight into the helping process.

Having emotional problems is only one reason to seek personal counseling from a trained psychotherapist. Another reason for personal counseling is the search for personal growth and superior mental health. If we spend many years and many thousands of dollars obtaining an intellectual education, why not devote energy and money to improving our emotional functioning?

I expect to continue my counseling sessions for several more years. After all, I went to college and graduate school for 11 years, now I seriously want to obtain the emotional equivalent of a Ph.D. I am willing to devote the time and money (above what my health insurance will pay) to achieve that goal.

I must warn you that psychotherapy costs between $60 and $100 per 50-minute session. Insurance companies limit the number of sessions allotted annually, in an effort to protect their bottom line. If your treatment goal is emotional growth rather than correction of a diagnosed psychiatric problem, you can expect very limited help from your health insurance provider.

Our emotional growth and emotional education are often limited to what we absorb informally from parents, teachers, relatives, and friends. These personal contacts may not give us sufficient opportunity to talk extensively about our feelings and receive feedback on how those feelings compare with what is really happening. After all, our parents, teachers, relatives, and friends may lack the emotional maturity to help us with our problems. Besides that, they are not trained counselors.

Unfortunately, at its extreme, emotional immaturity can cause failure in careers, family, and personal lives. It can trigger severely disturbed feelings all our lives. We can pass these feelings on to the next generation in the form of alcoholism, child abuse, or other dysfunctional behavior. Alcohol hides feelings. An inability to handle emotions can cause alcoholics to inadvertently teach their children to hide their emotions with alcohol, too.

Not only do we have very few ways to gain emotional maturity, but our society generally discourages people from seeking help with their emotional problems. If we break a bone or have heart disease, we can seek medical help, yet if our emotions need repair we are supposed to keep that a secret and fix the problems ourselves without outside help.

A primary form of assistance with emotional problems is psychotherapy, an educational process that teaches people to cope with their emotions after they have failed to do so on their own. It teaches people to handle their own emotions and relate to others. Unfortunately, most people do not view psychotherapy as education, but as a corrective process for people with some fundamental human inadequacy. This perspective discourages many people from seeking the psychotherapy they need to live happier, more productive lives.

Because of this popular view, people who receive psychotherapy learn to be secretive about it and often are ashamed that they must receive additional emotional education. (It's a good thing that people are not secretive and shameful about their intellectual and physical education!)

People who see psychotherapists keep it a secret, for fear it will reflect badly on them. It took me several years to develop enough self-esteem to be willing to reveal publicly that I am benefiting from counseling. I am only doing it now, as a way of encouraging fellow employees to benefit from a process which I find very helpful.

Other contradictions surround obtaining assistance with emotional problems. While our society views psychotherapy clients as crazy or emotionally inadequate, it applauds the psychoanalysts (psychotherapists who have undergone specialized psychoanalytic training) as wise and helpful people. Yet to become a psychoanalyst, you first must undergo psychoanalysis which is essentially a form of psychotherapy lasting many years. Thus, if you undergo a moderate amount of psychotherapy, you are considered emotionally disturbed. Yet if you undergo extensive counseling, you are considered very wise. That makes no sense at all!

While psychotherapy is a system full of contradictions, it is still a system that has helped millions of people. If your life circumstance becomes difficult, remember that a limited number of psychotherapy sessions are available to all state employees annually, as part of our medical insurance. Don't pass them up!

This article was first published in (date unknown) in DLE Update, *Sacramento, CA. Reprinted with permission.*

Helpers

Age 49

One of my colleagues noticed some time ago that a "strange woman" was driving me to work. I explained that I had hired a driver because neck spasms related both to cerebral palsy and to excessive time spent at the computer were making driving painful.

For many years I have hired "helpers" to do things that either I cannot do or that I hate doing. My wife and I discovered early in our marriage that we were both happier when we hired helpers. A spouse is a spouse, and that is the way it should be. Many people with disabilities find this to be true. That is, trying to relate to your spouse in more than one role can be both confusing and stressful.

My first helper (after I moved out on my own), wasn't one person; it was a whole sorority, and they related to me only as helpers. Thus, there was no role confusion. The day I arrived as a graduate student at Florida State University at Tallahassee, I introduced myself to a pretty co-ed who turned out to be the pledge captain of her sorority. She asked me how I managed with my disability and figured out that I needed help with errands, transportation, and typing the final drafts of term papers. Her pledges took care of these chores for me all year! The only chore I didn't ask help with was laundry.

For them to do my laundry would have excluded me from a favorite Saturday night dating activity in Tallahassee. That was to go out for pizza and then hold hands outside the laundromat while your week's dirty clothes co-mingled in a washer and dryer.

When I left Tallahassee for the University of Wisconsin, I moved into a boardinghouse where there were plenty of students to hire as helpers. And at the end of my time there I was enormously flattered when my pretty helper offered to follow me to my job in California. She promptly deflated my ego by revealing that California's high population of Mormon men, and not my charming company, had prompted her interest in moving out here. Three months later she married one of those men, leaving me to find a new helper.

My next helper was Ben, an engineering student from Iran, who successfully infected me with the entrepreneurial spirit. On his advice, I bought a three bedroom tract home and subdivided the living room and den into three more bedrooms. I shared the house with Ben and four other student tenants for two years and made a good profit.

Although there have been many helpers in between, my most recent aides were four Asian graduate students in computer science from mainland China. They cared for me in shifts at night following my surgery in 1988. While I slept in the next room, they sat under a dim light discussing a computer language called Turbo Pascal in Mandarin Chinese. I had hopes of learning Turbo by osmosis, but that did not occur. Either they were talking too softly—or, more likely—my subconscious mind is just as ignorant of Mandarin as my conscious mind.

Seriously, most of my helpers have provided the assistance that was expected of them, and many have also become good friends. Yet, as I write this I realize that they've also provided an additional benefit—20 years of supervisory experience. I must remember that the next time I take an examination in my agency's administrative series.

This article was first published about 1992 in DLE Update, Sacramento, CA. *Reprinted with permission.*

Solving Medical Problems
in Midlife

Age 51

There are coping techniques available to middle-aged adults with CP who have total body involvement. Although some of the solutions apply to people with CP generally, I write from my own 50 years of experience as a person with CP with total body involvement. No medical advice is given, as I am not a physician.*

This article was prompted by the findings of a recent survey** of adults with CP, which included a description of their medical problems, particularly those that developed with age. Although that survey was not designed to draw conclusions about the adult CP population, generally, it serves as a departure point for this discussion. Note, however, that even though that report prompted the present discourse, the opinions stated here do not reflect the findings of that study.

That survey of 101 adults over age 30 with cerebral palsy in northern California showed the subjects to have more medical problems than the general population. Half of the subjects were aged 30 to 39. Yet among the 101 subjects, 63 had digestive problems; 44 had bladder-control problems; 43 had skin problems; and many of these subjects had a history of depression.

One concern of respondents to the survey was obtaining appropriate physician care to ensure proper diagnosis and treatment for all medical problems. Obtaining such care can be difficult for people with CP who have total body involvement. They may have complex medical problems requiring care from more than one type of physician to ensure proper diagnosis and treatment.

These physicians may include: (1) a general practitioner, (2) a neurologist, (3) a physical medicine specialist, and (4) an orthopedist. Each of these doctors has all he or she can do to keep current with advances in his or her own field and will rely on the other three for thorough care within each of their specialties.

A general practitioner (or family practice specialist) can diagnose general medical problems and provide early treatment before such problems interact with CP to cause complications. A neurologist will address ailments of the nervous system. As cerebral palsy originates from nervous system damage, a neurologist is prepared to reassess the original injury in terms of current functioning and prescribe treatment from that perspective. Such problems usually originate in the brain, which is the neurologist's domain.

In some areas of the country, physical medicine specialists also have a vital place in this picture. However, some physical therapists question the value of the services of these doctors and find them to be duplicative and interfering. Of all medicine specialists, they are most likely to give advice concerning physical therapy, exercise programs, and equipment such as wheelchairs and walking aids. They can also relieve pain with electrical nerve stimulation.

When I was lecturing on Speech-to-Speech in Australia, I mentioned that physical medicine specialists would be helpful in locating potential STS users. The audience quickly informed me that there is no such medical specialty in Australia. I was so curious about that situation that I spent my whole lunch hour looking for such doctors in the yellow pages and went back to lecturing on an empty stomach.

Orthopedic surgeons can help people with cerebral palsy by surgically changing bones, muscles, and nerves to permit functioning and relieve pain. Orthopedic surgeons experienced in CP can now diagnose and treat structural problems in many children with CP, which may help them avoid the severe osteoarthritis, which some adults with CP now face.

Patients should not make assumptions about what any of these doctors can or cannot do to assist them. Seeking proper diagnosis and treatment is the only proper course of action.

Yet, following that course of action may not always yield the desired result for adults with CP and total body involvement.

The complex nature of the diagnostic problems of such patients may not be obvious to one of those four types of physicians when the source of the patient's complaint lies within the scope of another medical specialist. It is easy for one of these four physicians either to overlook the necessity for a referral or to refer to a local specialist who lacks the prerequisite experience for treating CP adults who have total body involvement. In addition, if any of these four physicians has insufficient experience and knowledge of CP adults with total body involvement (a likely situation in most cases), proper diagnosis and treatment may be impossible.

Diagnostic and treatment problems are complicated by the limited medical knowledge about CP adults with total body involvement. Such limited knowledge tempts some physicians to rely on palliatives, especially when they know the limited likelihood of being able to help such patients. They may overlook the need to consult colleagues or the medical literature. The situation is then worsened by the reluctance among some physicians to admit ignorance or fallibility.

Moreover, until recently, the limited treatment options for such patients often made palliative therapy the proper course of treatment. This limited knowledge and reliance on palliatives can unfortunately lead to poor treatment as a result of a self-fulfilling prophesy. In the end, the patient and the family must ensure that proper treatment is received. My experience has proved that the informed and assertive medical consumer receives the best care.

A bright spot in this picture is the current trend for physical medicine specialists to receive increased training in the diagnosis and treatment of adults with CP. Those who have received such training should be sought out by adults with CP as the focal point of their medical care. These physical medicine specialists will be able to coordinate care and refer patients to other medical care resources as necessary. In any case, the physician team member with the most knowledge and experience in the care of adults with cerebral palsy with total body involvement should coordinate the care of such patients.

In addition to physicians, allied medical professionals including physical therapists, occupational therapists, and speech-language pathologists treat people with CP. Personally, I have also been helped by other allied professionals. My acupuncturist has been especially helpful in relieving pain. Feldenkrais practitioners also successfully treat people with CP with total body involvement. My Feldenkrais practitioner provides exercises and individual treatments to decrease spasticity and increase neuromuscular coordination.

Adults with CP, especially those with total body involvement, may be prone to additional medical problems, not necessarily related to CP. One example is digestive ailments that may develop for many reasons. Lack of a balanced diet combined with difficulty in chewing foods that provide roughage are likely causes. Lack of the necessary physical activity for normal bowel function is another probable cause. Inadequate dental care and spasticity-induced teeth grinding can contribute to dental problems that make chewing more difficult.

Another set of problems that can plague such adults with CP are those resulting from poor dental hygiene. The physical difficulty in obtaining adequate daily dental hygiene for such patients has been eased somewhat with the recent availability of electric toothbrushes with rotating brushes. These brushes allow us to reach dental surfaces which our limited manual dexterity previously prevented us from cleaning. Even with the assistance of this special brush, seeing a dentist every three months instead of every six months is necessary to prevent cavities given my difficulty effectively brushing my teeth. For a long and healthy life, major dental problems require prevention or correction.

Some people with CP may also develop bladder or bowel problems from a lack of access to liquids or insufficient exercise to develop sufficient thirst. Lifestyle changes, which prevent such problems, are preferable to any cure. Proper supplements can help prevent constipation, but consulting a physician is a proper first step. One would expect nonambulatory persons to be more prone to bowel and bladder problems than those who can walk. Any change in bowel or bladder functioning should prompt a physician visit. Some nonambulatory men with CP keep a urinal handy to make urination easier. This helps avoid the temptation to delay urinating when transferring to a toilet is difficult or inconvenient.

Deteriorating ambulation is another problem that appears to be common in CP adults with total body involvement. For example, they may have increased stumbling, pain, or increased spasticity in leg muscles that may be traced to wear and tear on hip, knee, or ankle bones from an awkward gait that compounds with age. Worn joints may pull on muscles and distort balance. An orthopedist or orthopedic surgeon should be consulted and X-rays taken. Stumbling can also come from changes in electrical activity in the brain, and a neurologist can measure some of these changes.

Deteriorating ambulation may necessitate using a wheelchair. Manual wheelchair users should be monitored by an orthopedist or a physical medicine specialist for wear and tear of the wrist, shoulder, and neck. Switching to a power wheelchair can prevent further damage. Unfortunately, a power wheelchair limits exercise and complicates air travel.

When deteriorating ambulation impairs movement, other forms of exercise must be found to prevent muscle atrophy. The CP adult with total body involvement may have difficulty finding appropriate exercises. Because of awkward movement, the exercise necessary for good health and for avoiding atrophy may wear out body parts. Exercise in a hot tub or warm swimming pool may provide the necessary movement without excess wear and tear on joints.

In my own case, muscle relaxants such as Dantrium and Valium were used to combat increasing spasticity and deteriorating ambulation for almost 20 years. Meanwhile, the mental slowness caused by the medication hampered my job performance. According to the neurologists and physical medicine specialists that I consulted, there appeared to be no alternative.

In more recent years, Baclofen, administered directly into the spinal cord, avoids the mental effect and allows much higher dosages to be used to counteract tone problems.

The spasticity was caused by sensations from my hip radiating down and across my legs. Yet I had no hip pain, and that made diagnosis difficult. Finally an orthopedic surgeon with extensive experience treating adults with cerebral palsy traced the increasing spasticity to a severely arthritic hip. A hip fusion and muscle lengthening reduced my spasticity and eliminated my need for muscle relaxants. The clear head improved my job performance and reduced my anxiety.

When neurologists and physical medicine specialists were unable to diagnose the problem, my experience resolving my hip problem with the help of an orthopedic surgeon amplified the importance of the role of all four types of physicians in the care of adults with cerebral palsy who have total body involvement. This experience also gives people with cerebral palsy reason to remind their physicians that an increase in CP symptoms may indicate the presence of an ailment unrelated to CP.

Allergies present another set of problems which may be common among adults with cerebral palsy. These may cause a variety of symptoms, including headaches, stomachaches, nasal congestion, and fatigue. My own fatigue was traced to food allergies and alleviated by diet. Physicians specializing in preventative medicine or allergy/immunology sometimes prescribe this diet.

Depression and other emotional problems are also common among adults with cerebral palsy. Since treatment is effective in many cases, given the biochemical origin of depression, it is important to find a specialist who can diagnose such problems. There are also many medications for depression, but one friend complained that the kind called "tricyclic antidepressants" increased the spasticity in his leg (an extremely unusual reaction).

Living with the physical and emotional stress related to cerebral palsy can account for depression and other emotional problems. Counteracting these problems with stress-relieving mechanisms is an appropriate response. I control stress with diet, exercise, and meditation. Each person must develop stress-reduction mechanisms best suited to their needs.

Other medical problems that can trouble some people with cerebral palsy at various stages of adult life include speech impairments and drooling. These problems should be evaluated by a doctor and often a speech-language pathologist. Many people with cerebral palsy probably know how to speak better than they actually do. The opportunity to do some speaking in an isolated situation may be helpful. The stress of everyday speaking situations in which they are bombarded with the responses of others can prevent impaired talkers from speaking at their best.

For example, my speech improved in high school after I became a ham radio operator. Ham radio involves talking without the possibility of interruption, and that experience gave me a chance to concentrate on how I spoke rather than on others' reactions. Unfortunately, the improvement lasted only as long as I used my ham radio daily. Positive speaking experiences can potentially improve speech, as success breeds success. Tape-recording stories or using a CB radio are other opportunities to speak without interruption that may be helpful. Akin to speech impairments are the drooling difficulties which afflict many people with CP. Physicians called otolaryngologists have developed surgery to alleviate drooling in some people with CP.

One way to combat some of the medical problems described above is through maximizing activities that can contribute to good health. Like all people, those with cerebral palsy with total body involvement are generally healthier and live longer when the nonmedical aspects of their lives are active and fulfilling. A happy marriage, a rewarding career, and friendships have contributed to my overall health. The historic trend to isolate such people and deny them the opportunity to pursue these goals was a tragic mistake.

Everyone with a disability should be aware of the resources of self-help interest groups, which focus on various aspects of disability. Independent living centers in many communities across the country have helped people with disabilities live more independent lives.

I must conclude by addressing the concern which some adults with CP have about the possibility of CP-related medical problems developing in future years. The limited medical knowledge of the aging process in CP makes it difficult to address such concerns. Until the development of antibiotics, many infants and children with CP died from infections, particularly respiratory ones.

Those of us with cerebral palsy now facing the dilemmas of aging are the first generation to do so in large numbers. Like the pioneers on any frontier, our lives may be difficult and our challenges enormous, but we can take pride in knowing how much our efforts will benefit the next generation.

The author is grateful to the following people for their comments on an earlier draft of this paper. Eugene Bleck, M.D., Professor Emeritus of Orthopedics, Stanford University; Kevin Murphy, M.D., Specialist in Physical Medicine, Duluth, Minnesota; Richard Nisenbaum, Feldenkrais Practitioner, Sacramento, California; Ralph Segalman, Ph.D., Professor Emeritus of Sociology, California State University, Northridge; and Adele Spears, Research Analyst, California Department of Justice.

*Information about the medical aspects of cerebral palsy and related issues is available from:

United Cerebral Palsy Associations, Inc.
Seven Penn Plaza, #804
New York, NY 10001
212-268-6655
http://www.ucp.org/

**This study was sponsored in part by United Cerebral Palsy Association of Oakland, California.*

Unpublished, presented to a conference on aging and cerebral palsy, Sidney, Australia, 1997.

What, Me Paranoid?

Age 47

Because Peter Palsy, former chair of the Disabled Employees Advisory Committee, has teased me that I have been acting paranoid, I thought I had better check the dictionary definition to see what he meant. If I am paranoid, I had better learn to hide it so people won't find out.

Webster defines paranoia as "a mental state characterized by systematized delusions, as of grandeur or specialty persecution." Well now, I rarely have delusions of grandeur except for my fantasy about being "Ironsides" when I push my wheelchair. I have not felt persecuted since I failed a calculus course in college taught by a professor with such a deep southern accent that I could not understand him. But if I am not paranoid, why do I worry so much?

If it is paranoia, I'd be tempted to blame my father who always encouraged my curiosity and skepticism. In fact, last April Fool's Day he chided me for my lack of skepticism when I initially fell for a very professional news story on a public radio station saying that the United States had sold the State of Arizona to Canada for 3 trillion dollars. It seemed like a marvelous way to wipe out our national debt. Along the same lines, perhaps Canada would like to buy East Los Angeles and the proceeds could go to our department budget. Then maybe we could buy "electric eye" doors for the front and back entrances to make this building truly wheelchair accessible.

For a second opinion on my paranoia, I put the question to Peter Palsy. Because he's just out of school, Peter knows the latest theories. At supper the other night, a meal of squid, baked tortillas, and sauerkraut at our local Vietnamese-Mexican-German Restaurant downtown near 93rd and Z, he asked me what my paranoid symptoms were.

I gave him a few examples:

1. I am afraid to sneak out early unless my boss has left or is really engrossed in a conversation with a pretty woman.

2. I get uptight when a new data set does not show what management would like it to show.

3. My stomach starts churning when I cannot find all my cancelled checks going back to 1972, and my IRS audit is the next day.

Peter responded that I had all the symptoms of Anxious Sivil Servant Syndrome (ASSS). To confirm his diagnosis he asked me:

1. "Do you listen to the garbage trucks every Monday morning, and then worry that someone forgot to put the garbage out?"

2. "When your lastest research project is a week late getting approval, do you worry that maybe the semi-colon on page 89 should have been a comma?"

3. "When your wife is more than four hours late, do you worry that she's worried that you're worried that she forgot to tell you she'd be late?"

4. "Do you sometimes rush to arrive on time for a meeting only to find out that no one else has arrived because they are all taking a long lunch?"

Over spicy chocolate-covered rice cakes for dessert, I answered yes to all these questions. Peter then definitely diagnosed me as an ASSS victim and told me to quit worrying that I might be paranoid as that was just another symptom of ASSS. So there, Peter Palsy!

This article was first published in April of 1989 in DLE Update, *Sacramento, CA. Reprinted with permission.*

Experience with Aging

Age 64

Comment to a Friend, 2007

By the way, this week I saw the physician whose practice partly focuses on designing PT (Physical Therapy) /OT (Occupational Therapy) for patients. It was tough to get an appointment, as she only has a half-time practice and has an established reputation after many years of practice, just like your eye doctor.

She set me up with an OT and a PT who I will see on my return. I have begun using a transfer board to get into bed. She sees some of my deterioration as normal. I suppose that is because of the interaction of CP and advanced osteoarthritis of the neck.

My orthopedist told me that my osteoarthritis was inevitable given the nature of my head movement.

"The Lord Giveth and the Lord Taketh Away"

I am pleased that I have coping mechanisms and good friends like you who make life good despite these inevitable problems.

Chapter Eight

Assistive Technology— Telephones

The most satisfying part of my career has been the work that I do to help make telephone accessible to many Americans with speech disabilities. The following chapters describe my experiences using and developing telephone services. Who would have guessed when I first interacted with the Federal Communications Commission at age 16 (to become a ham radio operator) that I would again work with the FCC in my 50s and 60s to develop and improve disability telephone services?

Using the Telephone with a Disability

Ages 48 to 65

Introduction

People with speech disabilities (PSDs) in all states and in several other countries use an accessible telephone service. Speech-to-Speech (STS) started as an idea in my head about 1990 and grew out of my own attempts to be understood over the telephone despite my cerebral-palsied speech. I successfully lobbied first at the California Public Utilities Commission and then at the Federal Communications Commission (FCC) to require that STS be added as a service of the TTY relay, and I was privileged to help write the FCC regulations for STS.

What Is Speech-to-Speech?

STS is a telephone access service for PSDs that is free to users. STS provides human revoicers for PSDs who have difficulty being understood by telephone and allows many PSDs to use the telephone independently for the first time! Users access STS through their state's TTY relay provider. Current STS use shows that PSDs find it readily usable.

The FCC now requires that STS be provided nationwide. STS is available nationwide and in parts of Sweden. Australia has a permanent service, which I helped design when visiting Australia. New Zealand recently began an STS trial which may still be going on.

Who Uses STS?

Most STS users have cerebral palsy or similar developmental disabilities. Individuals can be understood by patient listeners with acute hearing who have training and experience listening to PSDs. Users may also access STS with a speech synthesizer or an artificial larynx. It is against federal law in the United States of America for persons without disabilities to use the STS system if they are not calling an individual who requires a communication assistant (CA).

The general public cannot understand most STS users' speech. Users may also have dyslexia or limited hand use (which precludes keyboarding adequately to use a TTY relay service).

Most successful STS users consumers: (1) speak well enough that CAs understand them most of the time, and (2) have the social skills and motivation to carry on a telephone conversation.

How Does STS Work?

To use STS: I and other PSDs call toll free to reach a communications assistant. We can call either 711* and request STS or we can call our state's STS 800 number listed at www. speechtospeech.org

The CA places calls for me and repeats my words to the listener. Users tolerate well the frustrations related to having a CA make calls for them. They like the increased speed of communications compared with TTY relay calls, which are cumbersome when initiated by very slow PSD typists.

STS is very much like the TTY relay for people who are deaf or hard of hearing, except that TTY relay users type to a CA who verbalizes their words and types their caller's words back to them.

We learned from initial STS trials that good communication requires that the CA and both callers hear each other throughout the call. That is why STS uses "cross-hearing" (my word), which maximizes communication by allowing everybody to hear each other throughout the call.

What Do Communications Assistants Do?

The CA revoices what the PSD says after every three to four words, a procedure that I adapted from face-to-face revoicing. CAs make callers as comfortable as possible even when the caller is not understood. After two repetitions, the CA may ask the caller to "please say that another way" or "please spell the word."

The STS CA: (1) expects to hear someone with distorted speech or a speech synthesizer and is therefore not shocked or confused by them, (2) uses earphones to eliminate all background noise, (3) has acute hearing and excellent receptive language skills, (4) can concentrate on understanding the PSDs words, as the CA has no interest in content and no emotional involvement with the speaker to distract her or him, and (5) can solicit the speech-able user's patience.

STS Training: CAs who worked on the TTY relay need additional training regarding the needs of PSDs to work as STS CAs. Audio tapes of PSDs are useful to train CAs; the tapes

teach CAs the "feel" for listening to PSDs. We taught CAs how to respect PSDs. Training by a PSD helps CAs understand their job.

STS CAs need to be aware of the push to get new consumers into the market, and they can be extremely helpful by showing top-notch customer service when any STS caller needs to use STS. Most of our CAs are highly committed people, but the one thing I know for sure is that if this is a first or second time user "turned off" by a gruff CA or a CA perceived to be uncaring, they may never use the service again.

Outreach

The greatest challenge for STS outreach is that there is no central source for locating potential STS users. Potential STS users have been identified one-by-one in order to build an STS user base. It is like looking for needles in the haystack. To supplement this approach, outreach workers telephone and mail flyers to medical professionals who work with PSDs.

Some potential users so fear using STS that they must be telephoned and/or visited repeatedly before they will make an STS call themselves. Family members and caretakers may require counseling if they feel a loss of role and power when PSDs start using STS.

About a half million Americans could use STS if they knew that it existed. Because of intensive outreach, California has more STS users than any other state.

What Users Say

I asked one STS user if she would attempt the same calls on her own without STS, and she replied, "Never in a million years!" Several employers of users say that STS improved on-the-job communication. One recent college graduate applied to law school because STS would enable her to telephone clients.

Dr. Judy Montgomery, Past National President of the American Speech-Language-Hearing Association, told me that STS relieved the able-bodied caller of responsibility for deciphering garbled speech and allowed her to concentrate on the content of the call. An aide in the California Governor's Office told me that he was impressed with the potential of STS to increase the employment opportunities of PSDs.

Note:

STS broadens the role of relay. Direct and speedy telephone access helps mainstream PSDs into jobs and many other activities. Such service expansion reflects the spirit of the Americans with Disabilities Act (ADA). The ADA advocates using new technology to benefit people with disabilities.

The ability to make one's own phone calls dramatically increases one's independence. Think back on all the phone calls that you have made in the last week and consider how much independence you would lose if you had to ask a friend to make each of those calls for you!

Next to earning a Ph.D., developing STS is the most exciting thing I ever did. Imagine my joy helping others overcome what had been my own greatest personal frustration!

Unpublished, first written in 1995.

Chapter Nine

Public Relations

It's very important for people with disabilities to cope well with the reactions of others to our conditions. In many ways, our success in life depends on our ability to motivate others to respond to our disabilities in a positive manner. It can be tricky to correct someone's unintentionally demeaning comment about my disability without alienating them. One example is my humorous response made to women who call me "honey" or "dear" in a demeaning way, as described on the next pages.

An Unusual Friend
Introduces Himself

Age 53

Missive: I wrote the following article for the August 6 (about 1995) <u>Daily Miracle</u>, the daily newsletter of Pacific Yearly (Friends) Meeting—a "miracle" just because it gets published each day of PYM.

As I came rolling into Craig Hall at the Pacific Yearly (Friends) Meeting (PYM) for the first time today, I realized once again that my power wheelchair, my unusual motions, and my slurred speech are not familiar to many Friends (Quakers). So, let me answer some of your unanswered questions and make it easier for us to get to know each other.

> "My name is Bob Segalman, and I was born with cerebral palsy, a condition usually resulting from a brain injury at or before birth which affects about one million Americans and is often accompanied by cognitive impairment. (My intellect was not affected. In fact, I have a Ph.D.)"

In my case, I did not breathe at birth (for some unknown reason) and the lack of oxygen damaged the part of my brain that controls muscle coordination and speech.

Let me tell you a little about my life now. I work full-time as a research analyst with the Bureau of Criminal Statistics (BCS) in the California Department of Justice. We gather annual computerized data on crimes, arrests, and other criminal justice activity from law enforcement agencies and courts throughout California in order to produce annual reports. I also advise my department on disability employment issues and try to open up job opportunities for other people with disabilities.

A most exciting part of my job is the four days a month I spend on loan to the California Public Utilities Commission helping oversee telephone services for people with disabilities. I help the California Relay Service by chairing its statewide advisory committee.

Other things I do with my time include playing Scrabble, and taking part in Sacramento Friends Meetings. I'd like to get to know you, so do stop and visit. If you have trouble understanding me, we can go into a quiet area where you can hear my whisper. Don't be shy about asking me about my life and my disability. The way I open doors for other people with disabilities is by telling people about my life and my disability.

Stemming Unwanted Endearments

Age 64

Many people with disabilities are angered by people, mostly women, who address them as "honey" or "dear" or touch them in what they perceive to be a demeaning way. One friend almost ran Senator John Edwards over with her power wheelchair because he put his hand on her shoulder when they were introduced.

My anger is not at people who address everybody that way as a part of their regional speech, only at those who use it as a subtle way of putting down people with disabilities. Beware, however, that some people with disabilities don't bother to make that distinction. Such endearments can trigger visceral anger, such as that triggered when you call black people by the "N" word.

Many offenders, like flight attendants and waitresses, I barely know. In many instances, I am fairly certain that they would not address an able-bodied man in that manner. I feel demeaned. Only my lover and my mom have the right to address me in that manner. Addressing me that way assumes a kind of power over me, and I only allow those two people to have that power.

Recently, I successfully solved what was, for me, an annoying problem by saving the following in my AAC device (voice output computer):

> "If you insist on calling me 'honey' or 'dear,' I must assume that you are coming on to me."

Generally, the initial response to my remark is laughter. That laughter solves a problem for me. After all, I can't be angry at people who laugh at my jokes. Sharing humor builds relationships, and building a relationship builds trust. Twice in the last month, female flight attendants have called me "Hon" at the beginning of the flight. Both times, my reply triggered their laughter and we joked together throughout the flight.

Chapter Ten

Words of Advice

Age 65

When I was a young person, I knew no adults
with CP to whom I could turn for advice.
Thus, I want to write a chapter of advice that
might be useful to young people with CP now.

Another reason for choosing to devote a chapter to giving advice is that, as a man, I cannot resist giving it. It's probably in my genes. Thus, my last chapter focuses on advice. If I were to advise a young adult with CP on the most important things to achieve in order to live a happy and productive life, here's what I would say:

1. Get as much education as possible. You may be forced to accept a job for which you are educationally over qualified. In addition, your disability may necessitate expenses that able-bodied people do not have. Increased education generally yields increased income to meet such expenses.

2. Choose an occupation that provides these things:

   a. Good job security. You have enough to handle without worrying about lay-offs.

   b. Adequate health insurance.

   c. Good long-term care insurance. CP increases the likelihood that you will need care from others as you age.

   d. An opportunity to maximize a 401k or a good retirement. Similarly, CP can interact with aging problems that will force you into early retirement. I retired at the age of 61 when I no longer had the energy to work a full day. (Now that I am retired, friends tease me for working a longer day than I did for the State of California. The difference is that now I only do work that I truly love and I have no commute to tire me.)

e. An opportunity to maximize the use of your skills and abilities while minimizing the potential of your disability to interfere with your job performance. As an example, I was very successful in my work as a researcher, as that work maximized the use of my Ph.D. training and minimized my need to speak on the job. I was less successful as a social worker, since the work did not use my advanced training and was compromised by limited speech.

3. Settle in a mild climate. Don't make life more complicated with the problems of extremes in climate. Be comfortable. My Ph.D. program was made much more difficult due to the cold winter climate. I completed my Ph.D. at the University of Wisconsin and had more trouble with the climate than with the curriculum.

4. Get an even-tempered, undemanding pet. Pets can be good friends, very comforting, and usually do not require you to talk.

5. Make good use of computers and assistive technology. It is well worth the effort to learn to use them well.

6. Be as independent as possible.

7. Find ways to cope with how others react to your disability. You may need a qualified mental health professional to help you.

8. Find a sexual outlet if you want one. God designed us as sexual beings. Living without sex can be very stressful. Many able-bodied people view people with disabilities as asexual; thus, many of us are raised as if we will not be expected to be sexual beings. If we want to have healthy sex lives, we must compensate for that lack of education and acquire healthy sexual perspectives. Some mental health professionals may assist us in developing a healthy sexual perspective.

9. Marry with caution. Be aware that your disability can bring to the surface psychological needs and behaviors in you or your spouse that can lead to destructive and/or codependent relationships.

10. Exercise and find forms of stress release.

11. Get good dental care. Determine if extra brushing and flossing are necessary because of limited tongue control, which can inhibit nature's oral hygiene.

12. Be aware of your anger. Have an annual mental health checkup with a mental health professional.

13. Join a religious group. Religion can be a source of support in troubled times, and people with severe CP can frequently have troubled times.

14. Build a friendship network, but be leary of asking extensive personal assistance from friends. It is better to hire helpers and let friends be just friends. Online friendships can be very rewarding since they don't require speech. Develop a good support and friendship network.

15. Learn to drive, if possible.

16. Be cautious about having children. They are expensive, time consuming, and can cause much stress. You may have enough to cope with in life without being a parent. I had no children and I am grateful that I didn't.

17. When you have muscle pain and tightness, determine if it can be attributable to deteriorating joints. I endured many years of spasticity and pain unnecessarily.

Finally, if you want more of my advice, e-mail me.

Bob

Bob Segalman, Ph.D., SC.D. (Hon.)
Founder of Speech-to-Speech

Speech Communications Assistance by Telephone, Inc.
515 P Street, #403
Sacramento, CA 95814

Call:
1-888-877-5302 and then ask for me at 916-448-5517

E-mail:
drsts@comcast.net

Website:
http://www.speechtospeech.org

IM:
Mensaman1 (in Yahoo)—the fastest way to reach me.